The Rise of
Major League Soccer

The Rise of
Major League Soccer

Building a Global Giant

Rick Burton and Norm O'Reilly

Foreword by Don Garber

Afterword by Mark Abbott

LYONS
PRESS

Essex, Connecticut

An imprint of The Globe Pequot Publishing Group, Inc.
64 South Main St.
Essex, CT 06426
www.GlobePequot.com

Distributed by NATIONAL BOOK NETWORK

British Library Cataloguing in Publication Information available

Library of Congress Cataloging-in-Publication Data

Names: Burton, Rick, author. | O'Reilly, Norm, 1973– author.
Title: The rise of Major League Soccer : building a global giant / Rick
    Burton and Norm O'Reilly ; foreword by Don Garber ; afterword by Mark
    Abbott.
Description: Essex, Connecticut : Lyons Press, 2025. | Includes
    bibliographical references and index.
Identifiers: LCCN 2024039702 (print) | LCCN 2024039703 (ebook) | ISBN
    9781493086719 (cloth) | ISBN 9781493086726 (epub)
Subjects: LCSH: Major League Soccer (Organization)—History. |
    Soccer—United States—History.
Classification: LCC GV944.U5 B87 2025 (print) | LCC GV944.U5 (ebook) |
    DDC 796.334/630973—dc23/eng/20241121
LC record available at https://lccn.loc.gov/2024039702
LC ebook record available at https://lccn.loc.gov/2024039703

∞™ The paper used in this publication meets the minimum requirements of American National Standard for Information Sciences—Permanence of Paper for Printed Library Materials, ANSI/ NISO Z39.48-1992.

To Barb and Nadège

"If baseball was built on radio, and football was built on television, then [American] soccer will be built on digital."

—Internal MLS prediction circa 2023

Contents

FOREWORD

RICK BURTON AND NORM O'REILLY HAVE IMPECCABLE TIMING.

The Rise of Major League Soccer: Building a Global Giant arrives in the midst of a transformational period for MLS and our sport in the United States and Canada.

In 2025, Lionel Messi—the greatest player in this history of the beautiful game—is in his third season in Major League Soccer. Our landmark ten-year partnership with Apple is also in its third season of bringing our league to new and larger audiences around the globe. The third edition of Leagues Cup—our in-season tournament that features all MLS and LIGA MX teams—takes place in the summer of 2025. Our thirtieth club, San Diego FC, began play this year.

The tremendous energy and momentum behind the league continue to build, and the eyes of the world are on MLS. This is all happening as the *Federation Internationale de Football Association* (FIFA) World Cup comes to the United States, Canada, and Mexico in 2026.

Rick and Norm's timing is also fitting because last August marked my twenty-fifth anniversary as commissioner of Major League Soccer. Moments like the publishing of this book and the authors' request for me to write this foreword provide an opportunity to look back, which is something we rarely do. At MLS, we are always looking forward.

But there is no question: we have come a long, long way.

It is hard to imagine when you think about where MLS is today, that in late 2001, MLS owners were considering bankruptcy as the league was struggling to find a path that would deliver on our original plan: to be one of the top soccer leagues in the world. Back then, we had just twelve clubs, five owners, and just one soccer-specific stadium.

However, thanks to the commitment and unwavering belief of the league's original founders—Phil Anschutz, Lamar Hunt, and Robert Kraft—along with the work and dedication of our players, coaches, league-wide staff, and our business partners, we *doubled down* and charted a new path for Major League Soccer.

During the last two decades, MLS has defied those who believed that soccer would never fully become a major sport in the United States and Canada with committed fans, in-depth media coverage, state-of-the-art facilities, and world-class players. We have proven the naysayers wrong!

Today, we have thirty MLS clubs, all playing in terrific stadiums, with most purpose built for the sport. MLS employs more than ten thousand people who have the opportunity to work every day in the sport they love. North America has become the most valuable commercial soccer market in the world. Some of the biggest stars in the game have played in the league—from David Beckham to Thierry Henry, David Villa, Zlatan Ibrahimovic, Carlos Vela, and Chicharito. And many of the best young players on multiple national teams (including the United States!) have been developed in our highly respected academies.

Bottom line, MLS has been a major force in the United States and Canada becoming important soccer nations.

How we got here is thoroughly detailed by Rick and Norm in *The Rise of Major League Soccer*.

As they document in the book, MLS has established many ambitious goals and worked collaboratively to reach them. The biggest goal was set in 2010. With an eye on hosting the FIFA World Cup in the following decade (the United States, Canada, and Mexico ended up winning the bid for 2026), I told reporters at the time, "We want to be one of the top leagues in the world. We believe that if we continue to be smart, focused, and innovative, our league can compete with the others. Ultimately, if we keep focused and continue to manage our strategy properly, we should be able to stand toe-to-toe against anybody."

And in many ways, we have achieved our goal. MLS has become one of the top leagues in the world based on the quality of play on the field, the size of our fan base, and the overall enterprise value of our league.

And some of the most important and innovative companies in the world are now MLS partners. You will read about our partnership with Apple, which changed the industry and MLS in positive and progressive ways. I believe the launch of MLS Season Pass on Apple prior to the opening of the 2023 season was one of the most ambitious projects during my tenure as commissioner.

Rick and Norm's book details all of this and so much more. Many of their anecdotes and insights may be eye-opening for you. As I've known from their work at Syracuse University and the University of New England, and writing for some of our industry's most respected publications, Rick and Norm are journalists and educators who know how to ask the right questions and speak to the right people. As a result of this commitment, their accounting of the story of Major League Soccer is one of the most authentic and comprehensive to date.

The story of the rise of MLS is far from over. We will continue to evolve every aspect of our league, both on and off the field.

I hope you will come away enlightened by the stories and lessons shared in *The Rise of Major League Soccer*. On behalf of everyone at our league and our clubs, I want to thank Rick and Norm for producing a book celebrating the incredible journey of MLS to this moment. It has taken the teamwork of thousands of people to reach this point, and I'm grateful for every single one of them.

The most exciting for me is that there will be more chapters for authors to write in the future. As much as we have achieved in Major League Soccer, the best is yet to come.

Don Garber
Commissioner, Major League Soccer
CEO, Soccer United Marketing

PREFACE

A Word (or Two) from the Authors

As sport industry analysts/observers, we know numerous soccer books have been written including *Soccernomics: How Soccer Explains the World (An Unlikely Theory of Globalization)*; *The Numbers Game: Why Everything You Know about Soccer Is Wrong*; *The Club: How the English Premier League Became the Wildest, Richest, Most Disruptive Force in Sports*; *Fever Pitch*; *The Real Madrid Way*; *Star Spangled Soccer: The Selling, Marketing and Management of Soccer in the USA*, and even *Among the Thugs*.

None looked deeply into the possibility Major League Soccer (MLS), armed with a massive Apple sponsorship, the impending arrival of the 2026 FIFA World Cup in North America, or the landmark signing of the game's greatest contemporary player (Lionel Messi by Inter Miami) could make MLS one of the world's biggest football leagues. Or a credible threat, within the next decade, to challenge elite European leagues (i.e., La Liga, Serie A, Ligue 1, or even the Bundesliga) for top players and the attention of global fans.

To that preposterous end, we wanted to dig into the slow-but-sure growth of MLS in North America and bring a wealth of industry experience that might interest (or inform) MLS fans and sport business aficionados. Most importantly, we wanted to detail how MLS Commissioner Don Garber has, for the better part of three decades, led the development of a global sports entity commanding intense attention from rival leagues.

Garber's arrival at MLS in 1999 (coming over from the NFL) followed the United States hosting the FIFA World Cup for the first time in 1994. His hiring and immediate strategic acumen set in motion a mesmerizing quarter-century transformation that took a sport (global football) few Americans followed closely or played seriously and, with calculated resolve, built MLS into a far bigger league now on the cusp of becoming a global juggernaut.

Simply stated, Garber's gritty vision and powerful focus on partnerships have effectively made "soccer" a North American sports priority. Additionally, Garber, with the support of an ambitious set of club owners, has provided the blueprint for MLS to sit at the same North American table with the National Football League (NFL), National Basketball Association (NBA), National Hockey League (NHL), and Major League Baseball (MLB). It also didn't hurt that global celebrity David Beckham joined the league in 2007, first as a player and then as an owner.

We think Garber's logical ambition is to make MLS one of the world's top three football leagues, and this book will detail how that could be achieved.

It all starts with hard work, ongoing political savvy, and Garber's good fortune that will come to significant fruition when MLS fans, soccer fans worldwide, and non-soccer fans see the United States, Canada, and Mexico jointly host the 2026 FIFA World Cup. That comes on top of the United States hosting the Copa América in 2024, the *Ted Lasso/ Welcome to Wrexham* factor, adidas's continued spending, the arrival of Argentine superstar Lionel Messi, EA's reboot of the popular FIFA video game as EA Sports FC, and two major FIFA competitions held in the United States in 2025.

Significantly, the June 2023 announcement that Messi, hot off his 2022 World Cup victory in Qatar, would move to MLS and play for Inter Miami sent shockwaves throughout the sports world. Social media exploded and soccer journalists found themselves in a content-generating frenzy trying to explain the rise of MLS. Just one year later, in June 2024, the CIES Football Observatory reported that Inter Miami's total followers on social media (Facebook, X, Instagram, TikTok) increased by 1,348 percent (or 31 million followers) during Messi's first year.

Global responses to Messi's announcement ranged from anger (fans of his former clubs) and criticism (targeting club officials of those same clubs) to curiosity (sport fans intrigued by his decision) to North American joy and even admiration from fellow players. Much of this attention benefited MLS.

Those factors, plus the meteoric development of the National Women's Soccer League and the ongoing strength of the U.S. Women's National Team (USWNT) and Canada Soccer's Women's National Team (CSWNT), have all aligned to heighten MLS's relevance in ways never seen in North America before.

The 2026 FIFA World Cup will certainly build a huge promotional wave advancing soccer in North America and MLS specifically. Already, MLS features three teams in Canada (Vancouver, Toronto, and Montreal). Additionally, MLS interest in Mexico was notably visible during the spring of 2024 when Soccer United Marketing (MLS's commercial arm) announced Pepsi brands Frito-Lay and Rockstar Energy would join with Mexican brands Sabritas, a subsidiary of PepsiCo, and Gamesa to sponsor the Leagues Cup that featured all forty-eight teams from MLS and Liga MX.

Apple's 2023 release of Apple Vision Pro (Augmented Reality or AR glassware/goggles) was met with high interest and a view it represented the computational device of the future. Although sales have been softer than expected (as of November 2024), the product's adoption (like the iPhone or iPad before it) should come, and the Apple partnership will continue to supercharge MLS.

We predict we'll see much more from this extraordinary partnership, such as what took place in March 2024 when Apple debuted "the first sports film captured in Apple Immersive Video [which was] available only on Apple Vision Pro (AVP)." Specifically, this five-highlight film provided AVP users a 3D, 8K, 180-degree field view of the Columbus Crew capturing their third MLS Cup championship with a victory over LAFC in 2023, with stirring narration from MLS Season Pass broadcasters Taylor Twellman and Jake Zivin.

When one stops to consider this partnership, ideas around future product development connected to MLS are endless. For example, various scenarios are conceivable where by 2030, stadium attendees start wearing Apple-designed glasses to instantly gain access to game data, highlights, and scores from other games.

These AR benefits may sound like science fiction, but the ten-year horizon of Apple's deal with MLS, coupled with the technological advances and adoptions expected over the next decade, make almost anything possible, ranging from virtual reality, holographic presentations, and enhanced artificial intelligence tied to retail sales/merchandising and transportation.

By talking to industry experts (both in soccer and traditional business verticals), leading sport media organizations, and corporate sponsors, we'll detail our reasons for predicting MLS's explosive growth and the growing levels of interest by MLS fans worldwide. In some cases, these experts have written insightful commentaries included in the book.

From a business perspective, we think the partnership between MLS and Apple will become one of the largest disrupters in professional sport history, or at least the sport–media side. Indeed, it has already influenced decisions by others, signaling the ongoing decline of linear television. This book will dissect that partnership (and others) and explain how the MLS–Apple partnership will cause global fans to see these two important brands connected at the hip for at least the next decade.

To be clear, this MLS story is not one of a turnaround or a sudden shift. In fact, the league has been growing on and off the field for most of its thirty years of existence. League revenues and properties have been steadily expanding in value and quantity, with—according to Transfermarkt—the total value of all clubs going from $150 million in 1997 to $5 million in 2010 to $1,330 million (or $1.33 billion) in 2024, an increase of nearly 800 percent in just fourteen years.

Technical experts speak of the improved on-the-field product today versus what was evident two decades ago. Further, the MLS Cup, the league's championship game, has become an important annual event, with the 2024 MLS Cup streamed worldwide and featuring big market teams in Los Angeles and New York. Sales prices of MLS clubs have also increased notably, as have the number of bidders.

Sponsorship is on the rise, both in the number of brands and the categories represented. Blue chip brands filled the roster of 2024 MLS corporate partners, including adidas, Apple, AT&T, Audi, Captain Morgan, Coca-Cola, DoorDash, Home Depot, IHG Hotels, Procter & Gamble, Target, TikTok, and RBC. In 2021, *The Athletic* equated MLS club values to high-tech stock prices, which are often overvalued. By 2024, however, MLS team ownership had become a highly coveted holding, with purchase prices and expansion fees justifying the valuations. For many, author Malcolm Gladwell's famous "tipping point" had been reached.

Today, MLS is already among the world's top seven European football leagues. In 2024, MLS had the second largest attendance—with more than 12 million tickets sold—of all soccer leagues on the planet.

We'll close here by promising to use a wide range of experts, dynamic charts, a controversial television series, a Spice Girl, management theory, diversity, great photos, city branding, video games, and a play on an advertisement familiar to old beer drinkers. If you like MLS, soccer, any of its teams or star players, or the sports business, this book is for you.

CHAPTER ONE

Conquering the World

The Rise of MLS

How big will Major League Soccer get in the next few years? Very big.

In fact, as many longtime fans have been predicting, MLS could get so massive, it will take its place as one of the world's most important sports leagues. This is not a question of MLS catching the NFL or NBA in North America but rather a recognition that European (or association) football in North America benefits MLS and places it at the same table as the UEFA Champions League, EPL, Serie A, La Liga, Bundesliga, and Ligue 1. That is, as a leading property in the world's most popular sport.

Combined, this seven-league onslaught (plus the worldwide growth of women's soccer and the visibility of players like Chelsea's Sam Kerr and Barca's Aitana Bonmatí) has made "soccer" the world's most discussed sporting code and one influencing the viewing habits and digital streaming of young sports fans everywhere.

At the heart of that growth sits MLS and as the 2024 season finished, it was more apparent than ever numerous stars had aligned to propel the league to new heights. The greatest player since Pelé (or perhaps ever), Lionel Messi, was playing in Miami as a part of MLS. Apple was streaming MLS games worldwide. Celebrities were flocking to see the New York Red Bulls or LAFC and streaming channels were frequently promoting football-themed shows like *Ted Lasso* or *Welcome to Wrexham*.

It meant MLS, with powerful teams in Toronto, Atlanta, Chicago, Los Angeles, Seattle, New York, and Miami could, within the next five years, rival La Liga, Bundesliga, or the Serie A; all European leagues that rely on the brand name prowess of no more than two to three teams per league: FC Barcelona, Real Madrid (Spain); Bayern Munich, Borussia Dortmund, VfB Stuttgart (Germany); Inter Milan, AC Milan, and Juventus (Italy).

As far-fetched as it might seem, this also suggests MLS's CF Montréal might quickly rival any Ligue 1 club other than Paris Saint-Germaine FC or that Inter Miami will become the most discussed team in Mexico, Central, and South America. Yes, MLS could become highly relevant in the French-speaking and Spanish-speaking soccer worlds.

This premise of MLS exploding in global visibility may seem, at first, unlikely, especially given the lengthy history of Europe's top leagues versus the short time MLS has existed plus the long list of failed soccer leagues in North America. The EPL, a descendant of the English Football League, dates to 1888 and features big international brands such as Manchester United, Liverpool, Arsenal, Chelsea, Tottenham, West Ham, and Manchester City.

MLS, on the other hand, was born more than one hundred years later in 1995, a decade after the failure of the North American Soccer League, just one of more than twenty failed soccer leagues in North America during the twentieth century. Simply put, at the time, soccer was very much an acquired taste in the United States (and Canada), and few showed any twentieth-century interest in making that purchase.

At the time of its launch, MLS featured ten teams and while it would quickly grow to twelve, it ultimately lost two teams after the 2001 season, bringing it back to ten.

As of 2025, MLS featured thirty teams and was delivering the third-highest average stadium attendance of any sports league in the United States after the National Football League and Major League Baseball.

Perhaps of greater interest is the fact that MLS was already the second-highest attended professional soccer league in the world and although it trails the NBA and NHL in television and streaming numbers, it draws larger in-person audiences than both leagues by more than four thousand people per game.

As marketing experts often point out, big name brands enjoy distinct life cycles (birth, growth, maturity, decline, death) and while sports leagues usually enjoy lengthy periods in the "mature" phase, certain entities, during their formative or growth years, generate spectacular growth rates, growing faster than their competitors.

For example, UFC—the mixed martial arts fighting league—saw revenues nearly triple in the nine-year period from 2012 to 2021, reaching more than US$1 billion.[1] Following a merger with WWE, as TKO Holdings, the organization is tracking to hit revenues of approximately $2.5 billion in 2024.[2]

In MLS's case, the "brand" is in a true growth phase, where the NFL, MLB, NBA, and NHL are mature entities trying to maintain existing fan bases while searching for new ones internationally by playing games in Europe, Australia, and Mexico or by using technology or innovative concepts like the NBA's 2K League.

MLS is a great example of a "growth" organization, and the primary reason for the league's growth may have more to do with the league's birth year and advancing technology than it does with expanding geographic boundaries or reaching North American population centers. A national footprint is important but global distribution (transmission) is critical. This statement is increasing in importance with each passing year.

Wireless transmission of content, as opposed to cable, fiber, or analog systems (requiring broadcast towers and TV antennas), means anyone, anywhere can "tune in" and watch games. That is, if they have devices delivering internet access, which more than 5 billion people on the planet do.

Here's an example of how to understand MLS's fortunate timing.

---

1. https://www.bloodyelbow.com/2022/6/10/23155850/documents-show-ufc-now-makes-over-1 -billion-a-year-minimal-costs-and-more-growth-expected

2. https://www.sescoops.com/wwe/tko-reports-2024-q1-revenue-of-629-7-million-as-wwe-out performs-ufc#:~:text=UFC's%20revenue%20for%20the%202024,Vegas'%20T%2 DMobile%20Arena

Back in 1995, author Nicholas Negroponte noted in his seminal technology book *Being Digital* that when the Berlin Wall came down in 1989, it crumbled five to seven years too soon because "it was too early to build an all-fiber telephone plant throughout East Germany (since the prices were not yet low enough)."

This meant East Germany, in leaving the Russian Federation to rejoin West Germany, would have been far more advanced in its communications capabilities had the transition taken place after fiber replaced copper wiring at an affordable price.

This is the same logic that benefits MLS today. Because the league's birth and initial growth came just before the advent of media technology expansion, it meant MLS was young enough, and neither its owners nor commissioner were set in fixed, traditional ways. They could afford to experiment with and adopt new technology.

In essence, MLS was "born" to take advantage of a global sport using worldwide streaming and digital consumption. So much so that the 2020s decade will be remembered as the era where technological advancement reshaped the professional sports world.

To provide context, MLS was just ten years old when Facebook launched. Since then, smartphones, video-on-demand, content streaming, generative interfaces (think Amazon's Alexa or Apple's Siri), artificial intelligence (AI), virtual reality (VR), and augmented reality (AR) are suddenly available for any entity working in the high-stakes professional sport poker game.

In 2008, Gladwell wrote about the benefit of timing in his book *Outliers* when he suggested humans are given gifts based on their birth year, birth month, birth order, and birth location. In MLS's case, and that of its long-serving Commissioner Garber, much investment capital was needed when MLS launched in 1995. Three of the other big leagues (MLB, NHL, NFL) had been around for more than seventy years. The NBA, launched in 1946, was the baby.

In hindsight, building on the success of the 1994 *Federation Internationale de Football Association* (FIFA) World Cup held in the United States, a 1995 launch into the sports world was ideal timing. Although expensive and risky (and by some estimates MLS's early investors lost more than $1 billion during the league's formative early years), MLS's owners persisted.

Not surprisingly, better financial returns were expected for a league born in the mid-1990s and not the 1920s. Then, as now, soccer was a global game, but the non-Hispanic populations of the United States and Canada had been culturally resistant to the game. The Americans, particularly, were seen as the last, and only, big country steering away from the sport. That began to change as the United States entered the twenty-first century and deep-pocketed tycoons began recognizing the realities of a global economy and international opportunity. Canada soon followed.

Said another way, if North American millionaires and billionaires invested in soccer, how could MLS fail? The answer in the 1990s was "quite easily."

Many previous attempts had nosedived and, indeed, for most of the league's first few years, before Garber took the helm in 1999, the business-side results were pitiable. Checks were regularly written to cover losses.

Since then, Garber's vision of expansion, the weaning away from the league's single-entity structure, David Beckham's arrival and ongoing involvement, the push for soccer-only stadiums, and strict fiscal discipline have brought MLS to a point where a technology giant like Apple and a global apparel brand like adidas would consider displacing traditional broadcasters and smaller brands for exclusive rights. Many of those decisions have come, not only with detractors, from owners and fans alike, but also from media outlets traditionally focused on football, basketball, and baseball.

MLS TODAY

To draw a line in the sand, or find the "tipping point" for MLS, it would seem everything changed when a historic distribution package between MLS and Apple was struck in June 2022. While terms of the deal were never formally released, it's believed MLS selected Apple as their technology/streaming partner (Season Pass on Apple TV+) because of a groundbreaking ten-year offer worth a minimum of $2.5 billion or

$250 million annually which could rise higher based on the number of subscribers.

That yearly outlay nearly quadrupled MLS's previous deals with Fox Sports, ESPN, and Univision that had generated $90 million annually. On those grounds, one could suggest it was Apple who selected MLS.

"This [MLS deal] is very important for us," said Apple CEO Tim Cook during a presentation to MLS players, owners, and media at Apple Park in January 2023. "It is one of the key things we are doing this year and for the next 10 years. We're now part of a family together."

Apple's continued foray into sports (they had previously created a smaller deal with Major League Baseball) wasn't surprising. As the Associated Press reported, "tech companies and broadcast outlets likewise see the value of live sports programming. According to a recent report by Parks Associates, revenue from sports streaming subscription packages is expected to increase 73% to $22.6 billion in 2027 after generating $13.1 billion [in 2022]."

Notably, the Apple–MLS agreement meant global soccer fans were able to "stream every single MLS match through the Apple TV app, without any local blackouts or restrictions." Fan access to games would be at a level never before seen. Further, at least until 2032, Apple's MLS streaming service would be included as part of MLS full-season ticket packages for each of MLS's twenty-nine (and potentially more) teams. Other firms have jumped on, like T-Mobile, which includes a subscription to MLS Season Pass on AppleTV in its packages for its phone subscribers.

The joint release included input from Apple, thus providing insight into the long-term possibilities. "For the first time in the history of sports, fans will be able to access everything from a major professional sports league in one place," said Eddy Cue, Apple's senior vice president of Services.

Cue was suggesting that anyone with internet access on devices where the Apple app is found, including iPhone, iPad, Mac, Apple TV 4K, iWatch, Apple TV HD, Apple Glass (projected 2027 launch), and Apple AR/VR headsets like Vision Pro (released in June 2023) and other partners (Samsung, LG, Panasonic, Sony, TCL, VIZIO) plus smart TVs;

Amazon Fire TV and Roku devices; PlayStation and Xbox gaming consoles; Chromecast with Google TV; and Comcast Xfinity, could watch games live when they wanted and where they wanted, regardless of time zone, location, or time of day.

"It's a dream come true for MLS fans, soccer fans, and anyone who loves sports. No fragmentation, no frustration—just the flexibility to sign up for one convenient service that gives you everything MLS, anywhere and anytime you want to watch," said Cue.

So what? How could this be the "tipping point" for a league that has been on a twenty-year growth trajectory? Two distinct benefits from this deal stand out to respond to this question.

First, the Apple package, virtually overnight (although the planning took years), meant MLS made the decision not to rely on a traditional TV network. This choice came on the heels of the NFL's announcement it would partner with Amazon for *NFL Thursday Night Football* at a reported $1 billion per year for eleven years.

Second, the value of MLS associating with the most valuable brand in the world, Apple, cannot be underestimated. This agreement vaulted MLS into the same stratosphere as other major leagues.

With Amazon joining Disney (ESPN/ABC), Viacom/CBS/Paramount, Fox, and Comcast (NBC) in buying NFL broadcast rights in 2021, the NFL, the most financially successful league in the world, started a media partnership journey that would generate more than $100 billion through the end of the agreement in 2033.

This is not to suggest there won't be growing pains for the MLS–Apple relationship. When the agreement was first announced, many fans balked when they learned they would be required or forced to purchase the MLS Season Pass on Apple TV to watch games. The NFL faced the same blowback with its Thursday night Amazon package requiring viewers to engage with Twitter in 2016 and Amazon Prime ever since.

Over time, though, fans of leagues have tended to make the adjustment rather than drop their affinity for a sport. Technologies may change but love of a team is a harder habit to drop. On the flipside, for some, easier access in formats they prefer may enhance their affinity.

It is hard to argue the Apple deal does not make MLS look smart, savvy, and modern. Indeed, prior to the Apple deal, MLS did not have the clout of the NFL or the NBA. As of 2024, the league has partnered with Apple's attractive digital distribution system, not a linear/cable network but rather a globally available provider to billions.

THE INFLUENCING ROLE OF GLOBAL EVENTS

At the global level, football has enjoyed a long and spectacular trajectory of growth, much of which has been driven by its signature events. Some might say it was best reflected on the field at the 2022 FIFA World Cup when an American team was able to stay with traditional FIFA power England for an entire game (drawing 0–0). The ratings for this game were impressive, with 15.4 million U.S. viewers watching in English on Fox and another 4.6 million watching in Spanish on Telemundo.

Perhaps most exciting for MLS and soccer in North America has been knowing the FIFA 2026 World Cup will take place in sixteen North American cities with the United States (eleven venues), Mexico (three), and Canada (two) sharing hosting duties for 104 total games.

Although not as closely followed as mainstream North American leagues by the non-Hispanic population, the United States played host to the 2024 Copa América tournament, perhaps South America's biggest event, where Messi's Argentina was the defending champion. That event, which concluded in July 2024, was won again by Argentina, beating Colombia 1–0.

Following Copa América, the cascading sequence of global tournaments continues with two events: the 2025 FIFA Club World Cup and 2025 CONCACAF Gold Cup. They are followed by the FIFA 2026 World Cup, and 2028 Los Angeles Summer Olympics (primarily featuring U-23 rosters for the men).

The hosting of these four global events will also coincide with the arrival and coming mainstream consumer usage of virtual or augmented reality technology, pushed initially by Meta and its Quest headsets ("the official VR headsets of the NBA and WNBA"). These devices and Apple's Vision Pro will allow viewers to attend games virtually in perceived 3D.

By early 2023, the NBA had extended its partnership agreement with Meta and Xtadium to give fans the ability to virtually watch games via Meta's Quest 2 headset, an experience allowing each viewer to "sense" they were physically in a stadium during a game. This kind of "engagement" by the NBA, a competitor league to MLS, represented the testing phase for new technology. By 2026 and the World Cup, soccer fans will undoubtedly have started to unlock the capacity for entering virtual stadiums.

In other words, if Leo Messi is playing and Apple is streaming, tens of millions will watch.

But what about the many MLS games when Messi is not playing? Will spectators want to attend these games virtually? Perhaps not initially, but the concept of virtual attendance will change rapidly and excitingly. It will become the sport consumption option of choice eventually for all sports and entertainment, not just MLS.

Currently, the "live" experience of attending a contest in a stadium is more dynamic than watching a game at home. There are sights, sounds, concessions, fan engagement moments that cannot be created in an individual's living room.

That presumption is about to change.

As technology advances, fans will soon sit in London while digitally traveling to Miami to see a game with friends sitting in Tokyo and Sydney. The time of day and the place where the person actually/physically sits, or stands, will not matter.

And this won't hold just for the individual.

Groups of friends from all over the world will find they can attend games, sitting together and, in turning to their left or right, see avatars or real images of their pals sitting thousands of miles away. This technology will be extended to corporate events, dating, networking, and business conferences.

The prospects are exciting, but the risks are high. Since MLS is in the growth stage of its life cycle, the arrival of affordable, bugs-worked-out VR technology, most likely by 2030, will benefit MLS. It won't happen overnight.

Technology-based acceleration will certainly coincide with the FIFA 2026 World Cup. But how will global football fans consume MLS games during the World Cup year and beyond? How much will the combination of the U.S.-based 2024 Copa América, 2025 FIFA Club World Cup, CONCACAF 2025 Gold Cup, and 2028 Olympic Games contribute to the league's growth?

Many believe that with Apple as a partner and Apple TV as the platform, technology will accelerate MLS's growth. MLS could be a leader in this area, particularly when one considers that many industries are struggling to figure out hybrid interactions.

Imagine a New York Red Bulls fan, sitting in their living room in 2027, but also simultaneously walking into the stadium with forty-year-old Lionel Messi and his MLS teammates. Could that science fiction be real before this decade ends?

Futurists and more than a few reporters think so.

The textbox on page 11 reveals a fluid reality where sport organizations consistently hedge their bets while gauging the rate of change around them, while considering how to respond or leverage new sports technology.

It brings up two topics that threaten every business entity: organizational inertia and resistance to change. Many CEOs, but more importantly, many C-suite leaders and vice presidents, are generally not rewarded for taking risks that fail. This means as technology races ahead of usage, leagues, teams, and sponsors can be slow to react, and leaders are fearful of trying things given the career risk associated with failing.

The prevailing wisdom is that major professional sports leagues are incapable of going out of business, which is, of course, not true. Just ask the investors in failed leagues or teams like the original XFL/UFL, NASL, and WHA, or the fans of long-gone clubs like the Montreal Expos, New York Cosmos, Seattle Supersonics, St. Louis Rams, Quebec Nordiques, or Hartford Whalers.

Interestingly, in MLS's case, Commissioner Garber and his media consultants studied the distribution patterns employed by the NFL, MLB, the NBA, NHL, NASCAR, Formula 1, and UFC. Each sports property revealed, during the previous two decades, the best way to

DECIPHERING THE APPLE–MLS AGREEMENT

Dave Bauder, a media reporter for the Associated Press, said in a 2023 interview[3] that "this strikes me as a very important deal for both sides. Apple is trying to get into sports streaming but is unlikely to be able to show what it can do as thoroughly with any other product as it can with this one."

"In other words," he continued, "breaking into the more established American sports means accepting limited packages—like Amazon's Thursday night NFL football games, for instance. This deal [between Apple and MLS] lets them work with an open, and largely untouched canvas. Apple will be able to grow their product offerings with MLS's audience, which in the United States only figures to increase, particularly after a gripping World Cup and the prospect of the next men's World Cup over here.

"And it's a younger audience, thus more valuable to boot. With the obvious exception of American football, many of the U.S.-based sports are more regional in their appeal—I'll watch every Mets game, and frankly don't care to watch the Rays or Angels. I don't know for sure, but I think that would be less of a problem with soccer in the U.S."

He went on to add, "I also find it fascinating, and a bit amusing, how streaming services have come around to appreciate some of the ways that broadcast and cable networks previously operated. In other words, they fully recognize the value of live sports. Some of the entertainment shows now have one or two episodes 'drop' each week—as opposed to an entire season. And, lo and behold, the streamers are airing commercials! What a concept!"

---

3. Dave Bauder did a sit-down interview with the authors.

reach a unique fan base was accomplished while rewarding stakeholders, including team owners or investors.

MLS signing Apple, ahead of other leagues with longer histories or larger fan bases, suggested a league commissioner who understood the contemporary media realm. Not engaging Disney (ESPN/ABC), Paramount (CBS), or Comcast (NBC) showed an understanding of the MMAANG acronym: Microsoft, Meta, Amazon, Apple, Netflix, and Google. It showed when the NFL chose Amazon (for Prime distribution), MLS followed suit by partnering with Apple.

Why are the MMAANG companies important? The short answer is digital efficiency. The long answer involves the financial reality of engaging fans with compelling digital access. A physical stadium has capacity limits on how many humans the building can hold. Those spectators generate what sport industry experts call the "per cap" or the amount of income generated per individual fan. For example, if a team earns $500,000 from game food, beverage, parking, and merchandise sales (T-shirts, hats, miniature helmets) from fifty thousand fans on any given night, the per cap is ten dollars per fan.

In the virtual stadium, though, capacity is limitless, and two hundred thousand spectators can attend the same game, each possibly spending three dollars for digital "skins," showing off their avidity for the teams involved. Or, if they don't want "skins," they pay ten dollars for the privilege of moving around in the virtual stadium and watching the game from different locations. Perhaps they get access via a product purchase or membership from a loyalty program membership? Suddenly, the VR per cap might far exceed the amount produced at the physical game. A sponsor's reach expands far beyond the seats in the venue.

This shift in the traditional team revenue paradigm makes a partner like Apple far more attractive to MLS owners. If Apple can design laptop computers, televisions, tablets, phones, watches, air tags, and headphones, chances are excellent the tech giant will also invest in augmented and virtual reality for their number one league.

Some readers may recognize elements of this discussion are seemingly drawn from Ernest Cline's 2011 science fiction novel *Ready Player One* where the hero, Wade Watts, alias Parzival, is unable to play physical sports in a dystopian 2045 but is able to enter numerous virtual worlds via his portal that leads into the Oasis. It's science fiction but set only twenty years from the release of this book.

Cline's worldview delivered a cinematic experience in novel form (later delivered as a Steven Spielberg movie of the same name) showing what life might look like inside a virtual galaxy where "gamers" from all over the world compete in games, mingle in lounges, socialize, or date. That *Ready Player One* came out in 2011 caused many to miss just how far ahead of the curve Cline was in predicting what the 2045 sports world might look like.

Less than fifteen years after the book's release, Cline probably could've set *Ready Player One* in 2032, thirteen years earlier than predicted. Support for that prediction came in 2023, when Amerco Research released data on the sports tech market and suggested US$61.7 billion would be spent by 2030, which meant the sector would grow at a 19.8 percent compounded annual growth rate for the next seven years.

See the textbox on page 14—to illustrate these points are six key examples of how technology is evolving and likely to serve MLS.

As noted in the textbox, another major accelerator for sports technology is the coming introduction of 6G wireless technology. As this book went to press, experts predicted the deployment of smartphone technology by 2028. Those same experts also believed intense competition in Asia could see 6G arrive as early as 2027. The expected transitional technology from 5G, likely to be known as 5G+ or advanced 5G, should certainly take place by 2026. That, too, will benefit MLS.

Augmented, virtual, and mixed reality will take on much greater relevance as companies like Apple release lightweight glasses that replace the human behavior of looking down at handheld phones. By 2030, huge swaths of consumers may read their emails, texts, social media posts, and resort to calling friends via a device designed to look like a very cool pair of sunglasses.

In the end, suggesting MLS could become as big as long-standing European leagues will seem far-fetched. But having a global partner as big as Apple and leveraging the global economies of scale coming to the nimblest of professional sports leagues, we believe that it is possible that MLS will find itself in the right place at the right time with the right connective tissue for a generation of tech-savvy fans who each day replace the baby boomers who favored MLB, the NFL, NBA, or NHL.

- **Artificial Intelligence, AR, VR, and 6G**—advances in technology are catching up to consumer expectations. Upsides are high for clubs, notwithstanding the risks associated with costs, loss of traditional jobs, infrastructure development, and implementation. Still, the upside of selling virtual reality experiences and VR merchandise may well offset the risks of adopting new technology as it becomes available.

- **Name, Image, and Likeness**—not specific to MLS, but the legalized movement enabling NCAA athletes to monetize their performances will eventually impact professional sport because more college-age athletes will arrive with preestablished brand recognition.

- **Data**—this is the daily practice now for sport. Executives are tracking everything and using data to inform all training and game-day decisions. They are also doing this both on and off the field.

- **Gaming/Betting**—it seems odd to consider this new or something to look out for when it is here and growing. This much is logical: MLS will fully leverage this sponsorship category (as a new revenue source) as well as benefiting from increased interest in MLS games from frequent sport wagerers.

- **Cloud Computing**—in the past, many stadiums and arenas dedicated entire floors for servers and other hardware to support data collection and technology. The growth of cloud computing allows for safer data storage but also opens space for other revenue-generating purposes.

- **Sensing Technology**—soon, cameras, microphones, and heat sensors will detect far more than a random individual walking along a stadium's concourse. Circa 2025, most public toilets could tell if a human was present. By 2026, experts believe, sensing or tracking technology will aggressively recognize the specific interests of a league, team, stadium operator, and fan.

Commenting on the Apple agreement, Commissioner Garber noted at the time it was announced, "People are going to say we are the smartest guys in the room, or we were a couple of years too early. The opportunities are endless, but it is an undertaking with many tests [to come]."

Those tests will dictate whether MLS, its executives, and its owners accurately predicted where the "ball" needed to go. If they got it right, MLS fans can expect MLS to get much bigger.

EXPERT PERSPECTIVE: KATHY CARTER, FORMER PRESIDENT OF SOCCER UNITED MARKETING

It was April 5, 1996, the day before the first game in MLS history. The weather was perfect in Northern California, and I was at Spartan Stadium [in San Jose] making sure we correctly painted the MLS logo in the center circle for the match.

Also on site that day was the match official, who told me that if we continued to paint the field, then he would not officiate the opening game as it was strictly prohibited by the "Rules of the Game." Thus, as we repainted green over the logo so the opening game could go on, the MLS journey of trying to find the balance between innovation and tradition officially began.

Behind MLS was a group of young, hungry, and slightly naive executives who knew nothing, or just barely enough, to not get deterred by the awesome hill we had to climb. At the time, none of us understood how fortunate we were to have a role in the development of soccer in the United States. We just knew how to keep our heads down, work hard, and try to prove everyone wrong who said Major League Soccer was destined to fail.

It was that unique blend of fearlessness, tenacity, and naiveté that became one of the secrets to MLS's success.

For me, a former youth and college player who never knew there could be a career in the soccer business, I was one of those lucky few young MLS executives privileged to spend the better part of twenty-five years helping build MLS and the game.

My journey included the 1994 World Cup Organizing Committee, the launch of MLS, a number of roles at AEG, including managing local revenue for six MLS teams, and ultimately, back at MLS, where we formed a new company called Soccer United Marketing—or SUM as it quickly became called. It was that last position with SUM that truly served as one of the innovative decisions that helped supercharge MLS.

In 2002, SUM was conceived during the potentially fateful meeting in Colorado where the decision to either shutter MLS or double down was made. Coming out of those meetings, the small but mighty group of owners, along with Commissioner Garber and Mark Abbott, hatched the plan of building SUM into MLS's commercial engine.

The idea behind SUM was to aggregate all the major soccer rights alongside MLS to represent to corporate America with a vision that $1 + 1 = 3$ and, by extension, grow the revenue/commercial pie for the sport and MLS.

The first acquisition of SUM was the 2002 and 2006 English language media rights for the FIFA World Cup. At the time, no English language broadcaster wanted to acquire media rights to games that would be played in the middle of the night in Japan and South Korea.

Thus began the journey of SUM.

By 2003 I had become a leading member of SUM and would lead the organization from 2010 to 2018. During my fifteen years at SUM, we managed or represented all the key soccer properties in the United States—MLS, FIFA, US Soccer, FMF, CONCACAF, etc.

Perhaps the key to SUM was our ability to speak about all of soccer in the hallways of corporate America. This was years before there were soccer specialists in media companies, agencies, and even corporations. We became that window through which corporate America began to see and understand the U.S. version of soccer.

In return, SUM and, by extension, the owners of MLS, made money. Perhaps more importantly, MLS was granted a strategic seat at the table of the quickly developing American soccer nation.

SUM became an economic and strategic catalyst for MLS (and its owners) and helped drive growth for the sport. Through the years, SUM evolved to include many business lines, including media, sponsorship, licensing representation, game promotion, and operational support. If we didn't do it already but a client needed it, we figured out ways to solve problems.

Today, many of those properties now manage their own rights, agencies have soccer divisions or specialists, and media companies are well-versed on the global soccer ecosystem. But SUM and MLS are still strategically positioned as the game continues to grow.

What started with a logo on the field of the first match in MLS history spawned an innovative mindset that led to the increasingly valuable MLS and the creation of SUM.

Looking back, it is hard to see the growth and the billions of dollars that have been invested into the sport, through infrastructure, jobs for players and staff, and engagement in communities across the country without Soccer United Marketing.

CHAPTER TWO

Soccer Is Big Business

So Is MLS

SOCCER, THE BEAUTIFUL GAME, IS BIG BUSINESS. SO IS MLS AND UNDER-standing the "why" is worth considering in the telling of the MLS story.

Soccer, as North Americans call it, is epitomized by its extraordinary moments. From the FIFA World Cup archives, many know of Pelé's spectacular and eventual game-winning goal at the 1958 World Cup finals, Geoff Hurst's hat trick to win England its only World Cup in 1966, Maradona's "Hand of God" goal in the 1986 quarterfinals, and the Messi versus Mbappé 2022 finals duel where the duo scored five goals in what many consider the greatest game played to date.

Of course, those are just four of the many moments that people from every corner of the globe have inscribed in their memories.

Even the most passive of soccer fans typically hold memories of special, beautiful games. Interestingly, it is not always the world championships that produce these memories. It could be an extra time goal when a favorite MLS club finally made the playoffs, or a daughter's brilliant cross to her twin sister that led to a magical sister-to-sister goal at a regular-season U11 game.

As anyone who studies marketing knows, soccer's global reach and local passion equates to real value for those involved. That, in turn, results in financial opportunities and rewards. Since the majority of the world's population forever carries one of those moments as a sacred memory, many are also willing to buy tickets, stream games, join leagues, buy memberships, purchase merchandise, support sponsors, donate to youth soccer academies, buy television packages, join fan clubs, surf websites, and follow social channels.

It means one thing. The beautiful game is big business and one of the biggest businesses on the planet. *Sportico*, a leading media outlet that regularly generates valuations, shared some impressive data in May 2024 on the fifty most valuable soccer clubs on the planet. Led by Manchester United (Man U), with a valuation of US$6.2 billion and close to $1 billion in revenues, the top ten were the household names of European soccer giants.

In addition to United, the top ten included Real Madrid, FC Barcelona, Liverpool, Bayern Munich, Manchester City, Arsenal, Chelsea, Paris Saint-Germain, and Tottenham Hotspur. The EPL's Tottenham, number nine on the 2024 list, held a valuation of US$3.47 billion and revenues of $721 million for 2022–2023. Interestingly, there was a drop in valuation to $1.77 billion for the eleventh-ranked Juventus.

Taken as a collective valuation, the top ten clubs exceeded US$47 billion in 2024. And, unlike the NFL or NBA, where there is generalized parity in value across clubs, perhaps due to a limited number of franchises available in a closed market structure, soccer is characterized by super clubs whose value far exceeds other clubs in their own league and beyond.

Actual sales (i.e., transactions where one owner or syndicate purchases the club from another) in 2023 supported these valuations. These include (1) a sale for a reported US$1.6 billion for 25 percent of Manchester United stock in late 2023 which meant the club had been valued at US$6.4 billion; (2) the sale of Chelsea for $3.16 billion, and (3) the purchase of AC Milan for $1.2 billion.

In terms of reach and scope, soccer/football at the men's professional level is—by a wide margin—the most vast and deepest of any sport on the planet. There are thousands of clubs and hundreds of leagues around the world producing tens of thousands of professional players. As an example, Somalia has four tiers to its professional league, while Zimbabwe and Kazakhstan both have three.

The FIFA Club World Cup might be the best example of the vast reach of clubs in the sport. Awarded since 2000, the FIFA Club

World Cup finals are contested by thirty-two teams, but those teams emerge from a play-down that spans the globe and is open to any club. Inter Miami and Seattle Sounders FC will play in the 2025 FIFA Club World Cup.

Soccer in North America: Why Did It Take So Long?

MLS, with its North American structure as a closed league without relegation, is operated differently than the open premier leagues in Europe. That reality leads to fewer super clubs and more parity. This may represent one reason it took so long for MLS, or the professional soccer leagues who preceded it, to prosper.

If we compare soccer to the most popular sport in North America, the NFL, the games are very different. In the NFL, action comes in spurts, with each play capable of a big moment, then a break in the action while the players on both sides reset.

This type of action actually allows for more than one hundred different "moments" in any game. It appeals to American and Canadian fans alike, and as a result the NFL has moved past baseball/MLB (USA) and hockey/NHL (Canada) as the preferred viewing option of many.

Soccer, however, by virtue of its nonstop style, typically has lengthy periods of ongoing play before a "moment" happens, often in an unpredictable way. Of course, to the dismay of many North Americans, the potential for a 0–0 "momentless" game is a highly possible outcome, which many traditionally found unappealing. Soccer also doesn't have the natural breaks North Americans are used to for commercials, snacks, phone checking, and the bathroom.

Not surprisingly, it's taken time for soccer newcomers to get comfortable.

Comparing soccer to baseball, America's No. 1 sport until 1965 (and still among the three most popular sports), it's possible to suggest baseball is closer to soccer in its style of play, with long periods of slower action, culminating with key moments, like a home run or a strikeout, to characterize the game. Typically, there are more "moments" in a baseball game, and a 0–0 tie is impossible because of extra innings that guarantee the delivery of a game winner.

Layer in the changing demographics of North America, with more and more people originating from soccer-loving nations and this discussion gets complicated, biased, and generates strong opinions worthy of academic sociologists. Specific to the business of MLS and to dig into its story, there are several key inflection points to highlight.

The MLS Success Story

The business and sporting opportunities for professional men's soccer in the United States have been under investigation from many perspectives for half a century.[1] Yet MLS is the first domestic league, after many failures, to establish itself as an important and "going concern" in the sports industry.[2]

MLS began its first season in 1996 with ten teams and will hit thirty in 2025. Early club valuations have gone from a few million dollars to a point where *Sportico*, as shown in Kurt Badenhausen's expert perspective later in this chapter, now values a select group of MLS clubs at more than US$1 billion. There have been challenges along the way, including the contraction of two clubs in 2001, but the historic trajectory has been impressive on almost every business measure.[3]

There are nuanced factors that go into a domestic sport league becoming, or seeking to become, a global property. In many organizational fields, growth or major changes are characterized by or rooted in key moments, often called inflection points.[4] Thus, in the era of wireless globalization, digitization, esports acceptance, streaming, social media proliferation, smartphones, and notable societal changes, there are still key points in time that can be identified as accelerated growth, particularly for MLS.

Researching the question, "What are the key inflection points in the history of MLS that were essential to, first, the survival and, second, the growth of the league?" brings into play both document analysis, including materials shared by MLS, as well as expert interviews with North

---

1. Warren and Agyemang, 2018.
2. Bennett, Vaeyens, and Fransen, 2019.
3. Bradbury, 2021.
4. Webster, 1965.

American soccer industry professionals. We, the authors, undertook this investigation with a given set of expectations, but ended up learning so much more.

The results of our investigation reveal that the 1996 launch of the league was ideal timing. Although expensive and risky (MLS's early investors lost more than $1 billion during the league's early years), the owners persisted due, in part, to the successful staging of the 1994 FIFA World Cup.

Interviewees recounted the profitability, sponsorship success, ticket sales, and media results of the FIFA World Cup in 1994 that exceeded expectations and provided the new MLS investors with the confidence to launch and stay the course during MLS's early days. Thus, 1994 was clearly established as the first inflection point.

In 1994, soccer in the United States was far different. It sat on the fringes, if not the sidelines, of mainstream sport. Only a small percentage of Americans could name any top global players. It differed for immigrants who came into the country with a passion for soccer and a willingness to get up early on Saturday mornings to watch games from Europe. For these fans, their affinity was 100 percent focused on where they came from and not where they lived.

Then, FIFA awarded the 1994 World Cup to the United States, over bids from Brazil and Morocco. Coverage of this decision included "dismay" and accusations of "bias" and "commercialization" by FIFA. However, most public reports and the rationale put forward by many FIFA representatives for the overall decision outlined the efficiency of the U.S. bid, particularly since all of the U.S. stadiums slated to host games were already built.

Attendance records for the World Cup were set with more than 3.5 million attending at nine different venues across the country, an average of just under 69,000 per game (the previous high was just over 50,000 per game for the 1966 World Cup). Of note, the FIFA Museum says it "is considered one of the most successful sporting events worldwide" ever.

According to a 1994 *Sports Illustrated* article, the 1994 World Cup attracted 32 billion cumulative television viewers, including 2 billion for the Italy–Brazil final. The economic impact was estimated at $4 billion.

The second inflection point came just more than a decade into MLS's existence with the signing of David Beckham. Beckham, a global celebrity in both soccer and fashion, joined the league in 2007. Numerous interviewees emphasized his heralded arrival, and the resulting game outcomes were vital to the survival of the league. Documented evidence of this is of high volume.

Notably, the first couple of years of Beckham's time in MLS did not go as expected either on or off the pitch. It was only in the last few years when he "bought in" to MLS, his teammates, his (new) coach, and his club that a significant impact was generated.

On this point, experts pointed to the confidence of MLS ownership to pursue Beckham, offer him incentives beyond what other leagues could offer, and a commitment over time. In simple terms, Beckham brought the league credibility and made the rest of the world aware of MLS as a potential place for elite players, more than confirmed sixteen years later by the arrival of Lionel Messi.

These first two inflections led to an MLS that is firmly established in the North American professional sport marketplace. As evidence, the league added at least one team annually from 2017 through 2023, with another (San Diego) in 2025. Since 2003, twenty new soccer-specific stadiums have been built to house MLS clubs, with two more planned for Miami (2025) and New York (2027).

According to *Sportico*, the average MLS club value should exceed $700 million by 2025, with twenty MLS clubs ranked among the top fifty most valuable soccer clubs globally. MLS clubs are collectively valued at $19.7 billion, more than seven times what they were valued at in 2013.

In addition, expansion fees have moved from as low as $5 million (Chicago Fire, 1997) to $100 million (Minnesota United FC, 2016), a twenty-fold increase, and then to $500 million for San Diego in 2023.

As discussed in chapter 1, the league's ten-year, $2.5 billion streaming deal with Apple from 2023 to 2032, that includes all media rights, including streaming via the MLS Season Pass, may be looked back upon as an inflection point. With the signing of superstar Lionel Messi the same year, another possible inflection point, the league enjoyed a double-whammy inflection point that overnight catapulted MLS once again.

The 2023 season set new leaguewide attendance records, with 2024 surpassing the 11 million and 12 million marks for the first time. Interviewees also reported that merchandise is up more than 40 percent, social media activity rose more than 40 percent, and sponsorship increased more than 15 percent in 2024 over 2023.

Another indicator of the growth and success of MLS has been the interest in celebrities from other sports, entertainment, and business to become owners. The table below provides a list of some of these owners currently in MLS.

MLS Club	Celebrity Owner(s)	Industry
Austin FC	Matthew McConaughey	Actor
D.C. United	Yo Gotti, Mark Ingram, Jerami Grant	Rapper, Athlete, Athlete
Houston Dynamo	James Harden	Athlete
Inter Miami CF	David Beckham	Athlete
Sporting Kansas City	Patrick Mahomes	Athlete
LAFC	Will Ferrell, Magic Johnson, Mia Hamm, Nomar Garciaparra	Actor, Athlete, Athlete, Athlete
Nashville DC	Reese Witherspoon, Derrick Henry, Filip Forsberg, Giannis Antetokounmpo	Actor, Athlete, Athlete, Athlete
Orlando City FC	Grant Hill, Tamia Hill	Athlete, Singer
Philadelphia Union	Kevin Durant	Athlete
Real Salt Lake	Dwyane Wade	Athlete
Seattle Sounders	Russell Wilson, Ciara Wilson, Ken Griffey Jr., Macklemore	Athlete, Singer, Athlete, Rapper
Vancouver Whitecaps	Steve Nash	Athlete

The Business of Soccer Today

Starting at the global level, soccer's structure and following is dizzying, far-reaching, and notably impressive.

Since the early 1900s, soccer has been organized globally as a single international federation, known as the *Federation Internationale de Football Association* (FIFA) that operates as the world governing body for the sport. FIFA has more than two hundred members from jurisdictions and nations around the world, is well known, and is one of the planet's most prestigious sports organizations. Despite challenging political scandals in the last thirty years, the organization remains central to the soccer world, holds enormous internal influence, and benefits from deep pockets that fund its orchestrated agenda.

At the professional level, FIFA[5] estimated in March 2024 that there were just more than 128,000 professional soccer players competing worldwide. In discussing global interest, it is challenging to accurately measure the number of registered and nonregistered players active in more than two hundred nations and jurisdictions, but a fair estimate would suggest the total number is multiple hundreds of millions playing in youth, masters, and recreational leagues or assemblies. Few would debate whether soccer is the planet's most-played sport.

On the spectator side, a 2018 study by Ipsos[6] studying the populations of twenty-seven countries found 21 percent of people reported being a "passionate soccer follower and will watch as many games as possible at any given time," 29 percent reported they "follow soccer, but will only watch games played by my favorite league/club and national team," 30 percent "will very occasionally watch soccer played by leading league/club or national teams," and only 20 percent did not follow the game at all. The fact that half of the world's population is either passionate or a regular follower of the sport, and only 20 percent do not follow at all, is unparalleled.

---

5. https://inside.fifa.com/legal/news/fifa-publishes-professional-football-report-2023

6. Ipsos (June 7, 2018). Level of interest in soccer in selected countries worldwide as of May 2018. In Statista. Retrieved March 10, 2024, from https://www-statista-com.wv-o-ursus-proxy02.ursus.maine.edu/statistics/868932/soccer-interest-worldwide-countries/.

Of note, the countries with the highest proportion of passionate followers in the sample were Saudi Arabia (41%), Peru (38%), India (26%), Argentina (26%), and Turkey (26%), while the lowest were Russia (9%), followed by Hungary, and South Korea, all at just 10 percent.

The U.S. results reflected 24 percent as passionate, 19 percent followers, 34 percent occasional, and 23 percent never. Canada was even lower at 10 percent passionate, 21 percent followers, 34 percent occasional, and 34 percent never.

FIFA's six constituent continental federations are listed and described below in order of their founding:

1. **CONMEBOL** (Confederación Sudamericana de Fútbol South America) is the governing body for soccer in South America. It is the oldest FIFA continental body, founded in 1916 and headquartered in Luque, Paraguay. CONMEBOL's signature event is Copa América, first held in 1916. The event, typically with twelve or sixteen participating teams, is one of the most popular sporting events in the world and crowns the champion of South America. The tournament has also been hosted in North America (as it was in 2024) and involved participating teams from countries outside of its membership. No team from outside of CONMEBOL has ever won the Copa América title, but Mexico has twice finished second. The event is held regularly (typically every two to three years). Argentina, led by Lionel Messi, won the 2021 edition. The 2024 version, held in the United States, was again won by Argentina.

2. **UEFA** (Union of European Football Associations)—founded in 1954, UEFA governs the sport in Europe and is best known for hosting the quadrennial EURO tournament, which rivals the FIFA World Cup for global attention and interest. Headquartered in Nyon, Switzerland, and representing fifty-five members, the federation is one of the most resource-rich and influential in global sport. The Euro, or formally the UEFA European Football Championship, is its major event. The most recent version, in 2024, was hosted by Germany and won by Spain, who defeated England in the final.

The hosts of the next two Euros are England, Northern Ireland, Ireland, Scotland, and Wales (in 2028), and Italy and Turkey (2032).

3. **AFC** (Asian Football Confederation)—founded in 1954, the AFC includes forty-seven members from Asia and Australia. Headquartered in Kuala Lumpur, Malaysia, the AFC's main event for men is the Asian Cup, held every four years, with the next event scheduled for 2027 in Saudi Arabia. The 2023 Asian Cup was hosted by Qatar and had twenty-four teams competing, with Qatar winning the tournament watched by approximately 1.5 million spectators.

4. **CAF** (Confederation of African Football)—founded in 1957, the CAF has fifty-four members, is headquartered near Cairo, Egypt, and hosts the annual Africa Cup of Nations, its biggest biannual event. The most recent version, held in 2023, hosted and won by Ivory Coast, involved twenty-four teams drawing 1.1 million attendees. Morocco will host the 2025 Africa Cup.

5. **CONCACAF** (Confederation of North, Central America and Caribbean Association Football)—is the federation responsible for the sport in North America, Central America, and the Caribbean. Headquartered in Miami, Florida, CONCACAF has forty-one members and was founded in 1961. Its premier event is the CONCACAF Gold Cup, a sixteen-team tournament held every two years with Mexico winning the most recent edition in 2023 held in the United States. The 2025 Gold Cup will visit the United States again and has been co-scheduled alongside the FIFA 2025 Club World Cup to further build enthusiasm for the 2026 FIFA World Cup and accelerate growth of the game in North America.

6. **OFC** (Oceania Football Confederation) is the smallest and newest continental federation. Founded in 1966, it has thirteen members. It represents most of the Oceanic region; however, the largest country in the region, Australia, since 2006, has been a member of the AFC. The OFC is headquartered in Auckland, New Zealand, and its Nations Cup, the federation's major senior men's event, is held

every four years with eight teams competing. The 2020 version was canceled due to the COVID-19 pandemic. The 2024 version was held in Vanuatu and won by New Zealand.

The vast expanse of the soccer industry at the national, state, provincial, territorial, and regional levels is perhaps the most telling aspect of the game's influence globally. As of 2024, FIFA featured 211 federation members. These are often called National Sport Organizations (NSO) or National Sport Governing Bodies (NSGB) and are responsible for a given sport in a particular jurisdiction (nation, country, etc.).

With government support and funding, the NSO is usually responsible for a country's high performance, development, and participation efforts. In soccer, these 211 NSOs include the very large and influential (e.g., United States Soccer Federation [U.S. Soccer], Brazilian Football Confederation, French Football Federation), to the very small (e.g., Vanuatu Football Federation, Surinamese Football Association, All Nepal Football Association), to the many in between (e.g., Canada Soccer, Egyptian Football Association, New Zealand Football).

Digging deeper, each of these—or most—NSOs build networks around state/provincial/territorial members, such as Canada Soccer, which has thirteen members, ten provincial sport organizations and three territorial sport organizations, covering each of the Canadian provinces and territories.

MAJOR LEAGUE SOCCER IN 2025

In Wall Street terms, MLS is a growth stock. In fact, two clubs were added in 2015 and from 2017 to 2025, the league added at least one new expansion team every year except one (2024).

If a reader imagined they were in the strategic planning meetings for the league in the early 2000s, they might envision a blueprint for the "ideal" growth rate of a league trying to match the other four major North American Leagues (about thirty clubs), club valuation ($1–2 billion per club), and media reach (national television visibility).

Realists (or cynics) in the room might argue such a plan was too far-fetched. They might bring up that only a few years earlier MLS clubs were failing, moving, or retracting.

As of 2025, it would appear the planners, dreamers, or optimists won. The rapid expansion since 2015 has led to a thirty-team league. Check off the "thirty-club target" box.

In addition, club growth has been accompanied by extensive building of new soccer-specific stadiums. Since 2003, twenty new stadiums have become home to MLS clubs. As noted earlier in the chapter, two new soccer-specific venues are also planned for Miami (2025) and New York City (2027).

On the asset value side, sport industry content specialist, *Sportico*[7] estimates four clubs are already worth more than $1 billion, namely LAFC, Atlanta, Miami, and LA Galaxy (winner of the 2024 MLS Cup). The average club is worth nearly $700 million, with twenty MLS clubs ranked among the top fifty most valuable soccer clubs globally.

A most notable *Sportico* stat shows MLS clubs are collectively valued at $19.7 billion, more than seven times what they were valued in 2013. Clearly, the values have quickly increased. For instance, LAFC's estimated value went from $475 million in 2019 to more than $1 billion in 2023.

Further, expansion fees, the amount a new owner pays the league (and other owners) for a new team, are also a key indicator of club value. To have gone from $5 million (Chicago Fire, 1997) to $500 million for San Diego FC is beyond impressive.

According to *Sportico*, LAFC led MLS in revenue in 2023 with $140 million, with the Vancouver Whitecaps, the lowest, at $25 million. Combined, the twenty-nine clubs generated roughly $2 billion revenues in 2023, a +27 percent increase vs. 2022.

Unlike the other major professional sport leagues in North America, all MLS players have contracts with the league (not their club) and are paid by the league, with teams contributing to this expense.

---

7. www.sportico.com; https://www.sportico.com/feature/soccer-teams-football-club-ranking-list-1234721408/.

On the television side, in addition to the Apple deal with MLS, ESPN (until 2026) and CBS (2027) have deals with USL Championship and USL League One. Further, these two networks, alongside Amazon Prime Video and Scripps's ION, have a $60 million annual deal with the NWSL that lasts through the 2027 season.

Analysts might assume as MLS growth slows, the league would logically move along the traditional lifecycle curve into the later stages of growth before moving toward maturity, where—with a thirty-club product in place—focus shifts to other marketing efforts, such as sophisticated ticketing efforts, merchandising, gambling, esports, and fantasy league engagement.

But maybe not. It's possible MLS is still in the early days of its growth.

Researchers like to tell stories with metrics since few things illustrate the success (or failure) of an organization better. With MLS data, it's possible to share the following data points from the 2023 season to show just how much business was booming.

First, both the 2023 and 2024 seasons set attendance numbers league records, with more than 12 million fans attending MLS games in 2024. Season ticket sales were 15 percent higher in 2024 (vs. 2023), with twenty-four of the twenty-nine clubs ahead of 2023's pace.

Second, the LAFC versus LA Galaxy clash in the middle of the 2023 season at the Rose Bowl, set the league record for a single game with 82,110 fans in attendance. The July 4, 2024, rematch did not disappoint with 70,076 fans in attendance. MLS also saw huge early season crowds for games in Kansas City and Boston (New England).

The third data pillar is sponsorship, where activation efforts by League partners are a key indicator of corporate interest and a necessary vehicle for reaching fans and new consumers. Here, both league (+17%) and club (+15%) sponsorship revenue were up in 2024 versus 2023, particularly in Canada (+44% vs. 2023).

Traffic and activity on league websites are also on the rise. League merchandise sales on MLSstore.com were up considerably (+44%) in 2024. Traffic more than doubled on MLSsoccer.com (+102%) and the preseason game on January 19, 2024, between Inter Miami and El

Official MLS Partners (Circa 2024–25)

Corporate Partners

☐ adidas	☐ RBC Wealth
☐ Allstate	Management
☐ Apple	☐ Sorare
☐ AT&T	☐ Target
☐ Audi	☐ Ticketmaster
☐ Avant	☐ TikTok
☐ Beats by Dre	
☐ BODYARMOR	
☐ Campbell Snacks	
☐ Captain Morgan	
☐ Caterpillar	
☐ CELSIUS	
☐ Coca-Cola	
☐ Continental Tire	
☐ Discount Tire	
☐ DoorDash	
☐ EA SPORTS	
☐ The Home Depot	
☐ IHG Hotels & Resorts	
☐ Michelob Ultra	
☐ Procter & Gamble	

MLS NEXT
- ☐ adidas
- ☐ Allstate
- ☐ Apple
- ☐ DoorDash

eMLS
- ☐ Avant
- ☐ EA SPORTS
- ☐ DoorDash
- ☐ PlayStation
- ☐ TikTok

MLS Broadcast Partners
- ☐ Apple
- ☐ FOX Sports
- ☐ TSN
- ☐ TVA Spotis

Official MLS Supplier
- ☐ IMAGN

Community Partners
- ☐ American Red Cross
- ☐ Athlete Ally
- ☐ Beyond Sport
- ☐ Canadian Red Cross
- ☐ Children's Oncology Group
- ☐ Green Sports Alliance
- ☐ Hope and Heroes
- ☐ Memorial Sloan Kettering
- ☐ National Coalition of 100 Black Women
- ☐ 100 Black Men of America
- ☐ Sport and Sustainability International
- ☐ Special Olympics
- ☐ Street Soccer USA
- ☐ U.S. Soccer Foundation
- ☐ You Can Play

Salvador's national team was the most active day in MLSsoccer.com's history, including 49 percent of the traffic on MLSes.com, the league's Spanish language website.

Fifth, on social media, the league is also as strong as it has ever been. Mentions across all of the league's social channels rose considerably (+40%), and club channels (+15%) in 2024 over 2023. As of June 2024, Inter Miami led all MLS clubs with 33.4 million total followers on Facebook, X (formerly Twitter), and Instagram. One year prior, June 2023, they had just over 2 million.

Sixth, the data points from Lionel Messi's move to MLS midway through the 2023 season were profound. The data spoke to Messi's massive appeal but more importantly MLS capitalized on his arrival. Both Chicago and Nashville, teams that didn't typically draw large audiences, reportedly saw gate revenues of more than $10 million after hosting Inter Miami. The attraction of elite global talent goes beyond Messi. Notably, MLS had thirty-seven players in the 2022 World Cup, which ranked sixth in the world in terms of league presentation.

Quite simply, the league was prepared to welcome new fans and did so with ticket discount packages, Apple subscription options, and dynamic merchandise options. In preparation for Messi's visit to Kansas City in 2024, the club moved the game to Arrowhead Stadium, home of the two-time defending NFL Super Bowl champion Chiefs.

While Sporting Kansas City sold more than 72,000 seats, more than four times what they could have in their home venue, they also helped facilitate incremental season ticket sales for other clubs, plus MLS Season Pass subscriptions on Apple TV and sponsorship sales.

Seventh, the Apple–MLS deal, described throughout this book, is evidence of MLS's boom. In 2024, Apple TV reportedly held more than 25 million subscriptions, including many season ticket holders with clubs who received streaming subscriptions with their ticket packages.

The expansion of the Leagues Cup is the eighth example of the MLS phenomena. Following prior iterations that were small exhibitions only, it was held for the first official time involving teams from both leagues in 2023. The Leagues Cup is a partnership between MLS and Liga MX, a leading professional Mexican league.

In 2019, it involved eight teams, but in 2023, the third edition grew to include all teams from MLS and Liga MX—forty-seven in total—and was won by Inter Miami. Perhaps most illustrative of its success, the League Cup returned in 2024, with the Cup now formally identified as an annual property. Columbus Crew won the Leagues Cup in August 2024.

With club valuations increasing, leading to incremental discretionary financial resources available to owners, higher expansion fees charged to new clubs, and increased attention from non-sport investment groups, the number of major soccer events coming to North America, particularly the United States, is indicative of the attention on this market and the sport's boom. The list is impressive: 2024 Copa América, the near-simultaneous 2025 FIFA Club World Cup/2025 CONCACAF Gold Cup, and the 2026 FIFA Men's World Cup. As evidence of the league's success, in December 2024, the MLS owners rewarded Garber with a three-year contract extension that runs through the end of 2027, the year following the Cup.[8]

Summary: Soccer and MLS are Booming in North America

This chapter set out to explore the growth of MLS and soccer in North America. Graphic 2.2 captures ten points of concrete evidence.

---

8. Novy-Williams, 2024.

THE 10 REASONS WHY THE MLS BUSINESS IS BOOMING

- Growing Season Ticket Holder Fanbase
- Rivalries that Draw Large Crowds and Media Attention
- League and Club Level Sponsorship Growth
- Quality Web Content & Platforms
- Vast Social Media Growth and Activity
- Attracting & Leveraging Global Talent (Messi)
- Long-term, Blue-chip Media Partner (Apple)
- New Mega-Events Emerge (Leagues Cup)
- Club Valuations Rapidly Outpacing Inflation
- Hosting Many Major Global Events

EXPERT PERSPECTIVE: KURT BADENHAUSEN, *SPORTICO* COLUMNIST

Major League Soccer (MLS) has long fought for respect on the global soccer stage since it kicked off its first season in 1996. The on-field product has improved dramatically, but almost all quantitative rankings still put the league outside the top ten global leagues based on talent level.

But off the field, no league matches MLS when it comes to franchise values from one to thirty.

Sportico's 2024 study on the most valuable soccer clubs in the world featured teams from ten leagues and eleven countries—MLS had teams from the United States and Canada. The highest ranked MLS club, LAFC, was fifteenth, but it had nineteen teams overall in the top fifty, nine more than the English Premier League. The nineteen MLS clubs were more than the seventeen total from the three highest-ranked leagues based on talent—EPL, Bundesliga, and La Liga.

Premier League clubs benefit from the league's massive television revenue which is partially tied to the final season standings. Last place Southampton earned $132 million from TV for the 2022–2023 season, while Manchester City pocketed $224 million at the top of the table. They also almost all lose money in a fight to not get relegated or to compete with their European rivals in Champions League.

In Germany, the Bundesliga's 50+1 rule requires club members to hold a majority of voting rights, and the league also has much tighter rules on spending to avoid clubs racking up debt or losing money. This has hampered the growth of revenue and franchise values, as well as on the field, noting Borussia Dortmund's loss to Real Madrid in the 2024 final, Bayern Munich typically the only team that ever reaches the Champions League quarterfinals. La Liga has dominated the Real Madrid and FC Barcelona on the field and with finances with Barca worth more than three times as much as Atletico Madrid, which ranks third in value among La Liga clubs.

MLS gives owners a chance to invest in the world's most popular sport in its biggest economy. The league provides cost controls, new stadiums, long-term owners, blue-chip partners, and a single-entity structure that fosters ownership collaboration and innovation. The lack of relegation also helps create a floor or "stick" value for franchises who don't have to worry about being banished to a lower division.

"While the motivations behind investing in a team may be similar, the strategies and requirements behind investing in an MLS franchise and a European football club will meaningfully differ," AJ Swoboda, managing director at sports intelligence firm Twenty First Group, told *Sportico* in an interview. "MLS represents different economics, a different ecosystem, a different time horizon—all of which present unique opportunities and challenges for investors."

A decade ago, it cost $70M to get into the league, while today the average team is worth nearly ten times that. The opportunity ahead for MLS has led to clubs valued at rich revenue multiples, which remains the standard that investment bankers use for sports teams, as profits can be variable, and in the case of MLS, are almost all negative after debt service.

MLS franchises are valued at 9.6 times revenue, with only the NBA higher at eleven times after a recent surge where basketball values doubled over the past three years—NBA teams sold for roughly three times revenue a dozen years ago. The NFL (8.8 times revenues), NWSL (7.1), MLB (6.5), NHL (6.2), Formula 1 (5.1), and Premier League (4.4) all trail MLS.

Scarcity has been a major factor in driving franchise values higher in the four biggest U.S. sports leagues. There are only thirty-two NHL and NFL teams, and thirty in both the NBA and MLB, while more billionaires are made each year. The average NFL ownership tenure is forty years, so opportunities to secure these assets are rare. MLS has fed off this scarcity to attract investors at lower price points than the multibillion-dollar outlays required in the NFL and NBA.

There is also scarcity in global football, but it works a bit differently. At the top of the pyramid, there are ten massive brands and clubs, not leagues, that are all valued at more than $3 billion with revenues that range from $600 million to $900 million typically. They are nearly relegation-proof and comparable to NFL and NBA franchises, although valued at discounts to teams in those leagues, as the economic model is much worse without any meaningful salary caps.

MLS fills much of the next tier of soccer's financial table with values that range from $440 million (CF Montreal) to $1.15 billion (LAFC).

The average MLS team is worth an estimated $678 million, including real estate and team-related businesses held by owners, according to *Sportico*'s latest calculations. Four clubs topped the $1 billion mark in LAFC ($1.15 billion), Atlanta United ($1.05 billion), Inter Miami ($1.02 billion), and LA Galaxy ($1 billion).

Inter Miami was the biggest valuation gainer from a year ago—thank you, Mr. Messi. Miami's value jumped 74 percent, followed by LAFC (28%), Austin FC (27% to $800 million), and Philadelphia Union (23% to $685 million).

Inter Miami generated $55 million in revenue in 2022 but will top $200 million in 2024 with a full season of Messi. Clubs have formulated ticket plans to capitalize on Messi coming to town beyond just the one game bump.

"You are going to get a lot of first-time people at a Kansas City soccer game," Sporting KC CEO Jake Reid told *Sportico* in a phone interview. "We are going to expose 70,000-plus fans at the loudest stadium in the world to the greatest player of all time, and at that point, it is on us to reach out and convert them."

Messi helped boost two league initiatives—the Apple streaming deal and Leagues Cup in-season tournament—that began in 2023, and MLS clubs now have an opportunity and challenge: how to lock in a portion of those newly introduced fans long-term with the World Cup in North America in 2026 another catalyst for the league.

Don Garber is keenly aware of the opportunity.

"It's really about, what do we want to be by 2027," Garber told the media in December ahead of the 2023 MLS Cup. "We're going to have the eyes of the world on us. The soccer market here in the United States is going to be exposed to the entire global soccer and football community. That is the pressure that we're under to ensure, as everybody's paying attention to us, what is the product that we can deliver?"

Sportico's valuations are based on a "control" transaction. That's where a new owner takes over, instead of simply a person joining an ownership group as a limited partner with few rights. MLS stands out from other major U.S. sports leagues for its teams' ability to raise funds at valuations well above what most bankers expect for a control sale. The Houston Dynamo raised money in 2023 at a $750 million valuation, including the NWSL's Dash, while D.C. United sold a small LP stake at north of $1 billion, including its mixed-use development around Audi Field. *Sportico* last valued Houston at $550 million and D.C. at $720 million.

MLS teams generated an estimated $2 billion in revenue during the 2023 season, up 27 percent compared to the prior year fueled by more games with Leagues Cup, the addition of St. Louis, and Messi mania. The league incentivized teams to increase revenue when it cut the share of ticket revenue the league collects from 33 percent to 10 percent. The intent was to reward teams who are making the biggest investments in their stadiums. The move juiced the revenue of clubs like LAFC and Atlanta United, as well as anyone who got to host Messi.

MLS clubs now have an opportunity and challenge: how to lock in a portion of those newly introduced fans long-term. The Messi, Apple, World Cup, and Leagues Cup quartet provides a foundation for the league to increase revenue and grow into its rich revenue-multiple valuations.

The clearest indicator that MLS owners are expecting bigger valuation gains is the lack of sales, as no teams have traded hands since 2021.

CHAPTER THREE

Don Garber

Growth-Oriented Leadership

IN OUR BOOK, *BUSINESS THE NHL WAY: LESSONS FROM THE FASTEST GAME on Ice*, we, the authors, offered a complete chapter about leadership titled "It Starts at the Top." This cliché about organizational achievement would come as no surprise to anyone who studies business. The decisions made in the CEO's office generally shape the historic success and financial sustainability of each entity.

That's what makes a chapter about MLS commissioner Don Garber so compelling and so important to the overall MLS story. His two and a half decades (1999–present) as the CEO of North America's biggest soccer league provides ample proof that the right individual, supported by ownership, equipped with a sterling vision and the courage to lead, makes a huge difference for a professional sports league.

But where do those traits come from? What makes an individual the right choice to run an entity with multiple owners and constant media scrutiny? How does someone come to understand an ever-shifting calculus and mechanics of growth and then pull the right levers to achieve historic outcomes?

For the outgoing young man who grew up in Queens, New York, with little interest in soccer, the relevant part of Don Garber's journey began at the State University of New York (SUNY) at Oneonta in upstate New York. Named president of Oneonta's 1979 senior class, Garber had majored in journalism and business and couldn't help but notice the success of his university's soccer team and that of nearby Hartwick College (also located in Oneonta).

In fact, just a few years before Garber arrived on the Oneonta campus, the Red Dragons reached the NCAA Division II Soccer national championship game in 1972. Hartwick, playing in Division I, would finish third in 1974, 1976, and 1980, while winning the national championship in 1977.

During that same time frame, the small town of Oneonta played host to three Hermann Trophy player of the year winners playing for SUNY Oneonta or Hartwick College over a four-year period. They were Farrukh Quraishi in 1974 (SUNY Oneonta), Glenn "Mooch" Myernick in 1976 (Hartwick College), and Billy Gazonas in 1977 (Hartwick College).

Soccer was so prominent in tiny Oneonta, New York, that the town was eventually selected to house the U.S. National Soccer Hall of Fame in 1999. It closed in 2010 before moving to new facilities at FC Dallas's Toyota Stadium in Frisco, Texas, in 2015.

If Oneonta's soccer reputation helped, the foundation of Garber's administrative success at MLS undoubtedly started during his tenure at the NFL, where he started as a marketing manager for NFL Properties in 1984.

During the next sixteen years at the NFL, Garber would closely study two of the most successful commissioners in professional sports history: Pete Rozelle and Paul Tagliabue.

Rozelle, who was named NFL commissioner in 1960 (at the age of thirty-three), after serving as their head of public relations and later general manager, transformed American football until his retirement in 1989. He was succeeded by accomplished lawyer Tagliabue who steered the league from 1989 until 2006.

Both men played significant roles in shaping American sport as it related to owner-player profit sharing, media rights negotiations, expansion, legal challenges, collective bargaining agreements with unions (the powerful NFLPA), new marketing concepts (e.g., the Super Bowl, *Monday Night Football*), rule changes, the creation of rules, and even the merger of two leagues (the American Football League was absorbed by the NFL in 1970).

Garber was there for much of it, and by 1992 was designing numerous special events for television or, perhaps more importantly, for the NFL's growing list of sponsors.

During the 1980s, the NFL, serving as an umbrella organization for its member clubs, was still embryonic in its ability to secure national sponsorships that its teams would acknowledge and promote. At the time, NFL clubs existed in a world where they expected to "keep what they caught" locally. They might share national broadcast revenues but when it came to stadium sponsor deals (or soda and beer pouring rights), those dollars stayed with the local owner.

That began to change in 1995 when Visa was signed as the official credit card of the NFL. The scales tipped even further in 1996 when Sprint Corp. (a telecommunications company from Overland Park, Kansas) announced it would pay the NFL a then staggering $100 million for a three-year sponsorship that eventually placed Sprint logos on coaches' headsets.

In other words, NFL sponsors, and their on-air NFL-themed advertising (not to mention massive retail activation) began generating significant revenue and visibility for NFL owners who chose to share sponsorship revenue equally regardless of market size.

During Garber's time with NFL Properties (the marketing arm of the league) the NFL was not only mastering the art of selling the league's collective intellectual property (IP), but also upping the fan engagement game of each NFL team in their respective local markets.

Garber's later years saw his rise to the rank of senior vice president but more importantly, he became managing director of NFL International which included responsibility for NFL Europe.

To some, the thought of the NFL exploring the development of fan bases in London, Berlin, Frankfurt, Amsterdam, Barcelona, Scotland (both Edinburgh and Glasgow), and Düsseldorf (the Rhein Fire) would seem unusual if not, at the time, sacrilegious.

The NFL was America's largest professional league. Owner profitability and player salaries were the best in the world. Why would the league invest resources in Europe?

The answer lies in part with Garber's understanding of population forces beginning to shape the global sports ecosystem. If the NFL could develop a new product (NFL Europe, originally known as the World League of American Football) in new markets (Europe), it could potentially achieve diversification (a key strategic planning concept).

It's clear Garber understood how global economies of scale were relevant for the sports league of the future. While the NFL would eventually retreat from trying to sustain a league in Europe (replacing it with regular season games), Garber was introduced to the significant appeal generated by the largest soccer teams in the English Premier League, Germany's Bundesliga and Spain's La Liga.

All of Garber's NFL experience and training made him an ideal candidate for the vacancy that was created with the departure of Doug Logan, MLS's first commissioner. Logan had been installed as the league's chief steward in 1995. While he and the MLS staff would be named as *Sports Business Daily*'s 1996 Sports Industrialist of the Year, by 1999, MLS owner losses were piling up. Media reports six years later suggested owners had collectively lost $250 million during the first five years of league operations (Eligon, 2005).

MLS' most visible owners, Phil Anschutz, Lamar Hunt, and Robert Kraft, did not want to keep bankrolling an investment that was showing no signs of generating an acceptable return on their investment. A change was needed, and the search began. MLS's owners were obligated to find a soccer visionary who could break bread with billionaires while navigating North America's media waters.

Enter Garber, a sharp-eyed NFL veteran with international experience and an understanding of just how maligned MLS looked in the eyes of soccer purists, European league administrators, FIFA, the media, and American sports fans. Things needed to change.

Logan had done some very heavy lifting to get MLS off the ground following the success of the 1994 FIFA World Cup, but the product on the field was inferior, the stadiums were built for other sports, the rules did not align with the rest of the world, and coverage of the league was all but nonexistent.

It would be simple in a book lauding the rise of MLS to suggest Garber entered the commissioner's suite, saw the problem, snapped his fingers, and within a year or two the problems were solved.

In fact, like most hard-won victories in life, Garber needed to eat the elephantine MLS problems he inherited, one hard-to-swallow gulp at a time.

Still, a listing here, cribbed (and modified) from Wikipedia's entry for Garber, shows a wide range of achievements under the following headings:

- Orchestrated Expansion (including a move into Canada)
- The Construction of Purpose-built Stadiums
- The Creation of Soccer United Marketing (SUM)
- The Implementation of a Designated Player Rule
- Collecting a Galaxy of Twenty-First-Century Owners (David Beckham, Magic Johnson, Mia Hamm Garciaparra, Jorge Mas, Will Ferrell, Reese Witherspoon, Red Bull GmbH, City Football Group, Drew Carey, Steve Nash, Patrick Mahomes, and Peter Guber)
- The Development of Team-Specific Youth Academies
- Media Rights Deals (most notably a ten-year $2.5 billion partnership with Apple)
- Sponsorship Agreements with the World's Biggest Brands
- Philanthropy via MLS Works
- A Commitment to Diversity (including loans from Black-owned banks)

The list above doesn't do justice to Garber's tireless and authentic efforts to build MLS into one of North America's most prominent leagues, and his achievements won't change the nature of fans who, regardless of what their favorite league is, find fault with commissioners. It is with certainty that one can say that his owners must be most pleased with his results.

League CEOs are often unpopular with fans because their favorite teams lose or because a hated rival club signs a superstar, and another team doesn't. Fans like complaining about when games are broadcast, what streaming system is favored (or not), the fact certain teams always do well (and others don't), their perception player drafts are rigged, or that the commissioner is paid too much.

While all of the above may be true about human behavior (and fans always have the right to boo), it's certain Garber's steady hand on the MLS tiller has brought the league from the brink of bankruptcy (and another failed North American professional men's soccer league) to a point where MLS routinely features sold out stadiums, dynamic play, technology advantages (that will continue to grow between 2025 and 2033), and acceptance by FIFA as one of the world's top leagues.

Nowhere was this more apparent than the historic April 2024 visit by FIFA president Gianni Infantino, who came to Los Angeles to meet with MLS's leadership (Tenorio, 2024) in advance of the FIFA 2026 World Cup.

"It's the first time in 29 years that a FIFA president has come to an MLS board meeting and I think it speaks to or underscores the importance of the North American soccer market and FIFA is embracing the opportunity here to grow the game," Garber told *The Athletic*. "And it's exciting to see the enthusiasm that exists both at the FIFA level and at the CONCACAF level with where we are today, but probably most importantly, what potential we have to make soccer the preeminent sport in this country."

Garber's enthusiasm for MLS's future did not stop there.

"Gianni set up at the dais and just expressed his views about where the sport is in our country, his views about Major League Soccer and the impact that we've made in growing the game, both at the fan level which has been significant, but certainly our commitment and investment in infrastructure and growing the supporter culture," Garber added. "And I think he has very strong views that this is just the beginning of a journey where MLS can continue to evolve and grow with the right level of investment and the right level of support to reach really tremendous new heights."

Sports Business Journal even reported sources indicated Infantino "spoke about his belief that MLS can be one of the best leagues in the world" but to "reach those goals, owners would have to increase their investment, pointing especially to academy development and the first-team rosters."

Additionally, "Infantino said he had 'been impressed with the [MLS] owners' passion and commitment to grow the game, and the growth of fan bases, [soccer] stadiums and infrastructure around MLS.'"

A visit by a European dignitary to meet executives involved in running a league long looked down upon by Europeans may not yet register on the American spectator radar but the truth is simple: the amazing growth of MLS during the last twenty-six years is due to thousands of people (including longtime MLS president and deputy commissioner Mark Abbott, who pens the afterword in this book) but if recognition is warranted, it starts at the top with Don Garber. Perhaps the most telling demonstration of MLS's success under Garber is the aforementioned 12+ million ticket buyers to MLS games in 2024. The chart below showcases this increase and MLS's place as the second highest drawing soccer league in the world.

League	Total Attendance	Season
Premier League	14,673,035	2023–2024
MLS	*12,131,314*	*2024*
Bundesliga (Germany)	12,079,622	2023–2024
Serie A (Italy)	11,690,320	2023–2024
La Liga (Spain)	10,716,855	2023–2024
Brazil	10,270,564	2023
Ligue 1 (France)	8,405,514	2023–2024
LIGA MX (Mexico)	6,972,261	2023–2024

Expert Perspective: David Sternberg, cohead of media consulting at Range Sports, Fox Soccer Channel, and MLS

After working at the 1994 World Cup, I spent a couple of years at a consulting firm, then I wound up being involved in Fox Sports from 1998 to 2002. During that time we became a partner of the league with Fox Soccer Channel, Don Garber became MLS commissioner.

Fox became a very meaningful addition to MLS's success as it allowed MLS to reach a very soccer-savvy fan base, which helped grow the interest. Today, Fox is still a partner.

MLS was on ESPN at the time [late 1990s], but it was one of dozens of sports and leagues that were on that channel. At Fox, we were doing soccer 24/7 and we even had a nightly news show that was soccer highlights, news, and more devoted to soccer. This was in the pre-streaming era, and it was not like you could go on to your phone or PC and watch clips all day long. That meant we were an important lever to reach that devoted soccer fan.

Looking back, it was a great partnership.

At Fox, we had games and a dedicated *MLS Wrap* highlight show every weekend, which was the first—I think—show of that type. We paid a rights fee to MLS, which may be the first time that happened, and we were very big supporters of the league and soccer.

That was a tough time, as the league contracted a couple of clubs in 2002, but I think we played a small part in helping sustain the league and getting them through that tough period before the era of the soccer-only stadiums and the David Beckham signing. Success has continued ever since, and Fox played a part.

CHAPTER FOUR

How MLS Altered the Failure Trend in North America

THIS CHAPTER'S PRIMARY VIEW IS THAT LEO MESSI'S ARRIVAL IN MLS is not about Messi vaulting the league to the next level, but about MLS building to a level where a player like Messi, fresh off a World Cup victory, chose to come to the United States over other highly lucrative alternatives, including (reportedly) Saudi Arabia or a return to Barcelona.

MLS has survived where so many others failed to be a profitable, growing professional men's soccer league in North America. To grow from ten clubs in its first two seasons (1996 and 1997) to thirty is no small feat. Additionally, MLS has dealt with only three exits: the Tampa Bay Mutiny and Miami Fusion in 2001 and Chivas USA in 2014. That's twenty-three new clubs launched against three exits in twenty-nine years—a pretty good track record.

In 2024, *Sports Business Journal* reported MLS club revenues were reaching unprecedented levels, due to (1) the league reducing its "tax" on ticket revenues to 10 percent from 33 percent, leaving more resources at the club level, and (2) the impact of Lionel Messi joining the league, where clubs could generate excess revenues from his visits. For instance, in early April 2024, Sporting KC hosted Inter Miami in an MLS regular season game in an NFL stadium as opposed to their regular, soccer-specific venue (capacity 18,500). Total attendance for the game, won by Messi and Miami, was more than 72,000.

A Quick History Lesson of New Entrant Equity Ownership

Perhaps the best way to show the success of the league, beyond the high ratio of entrants to exits, is the increasing cost for new owners of clubs to purchase equity. A variety of reports (ESPN, *Forbes*, *New York Times*, etc.) over the past twenty-five years have suggested the fees paid by club operators in 1996 for the ten initial clubs were $5 million each.

That same price was reportedly the fee for Chicago in 1998 and Houston (relocation of San Jose) in 2006, with Miami (Fusion) paying a reported $20 million in 1998. Prices boomeranged backward when Chivas USA and Real Salt Lake both reportedly spent $7.5 million for expansion teams in 2005.

In 2007, the cost of equity ownership in a new entrant started increasing and it hasn't stopped since. Toronto (2007) went for $10 million, San Jose (2008) $20 million, before Seattle (2009) and Philadelphia (2010) came in at $30 million. The price tag jumped to $35 million for Portland and Vancouver in 2011, and $40 million for Montreal in 2012.

Beginning in 2015, equity fees jumped to new levels, with $100 million (New York City FC) and $70 million for Orlando City FC in 2015. Atlanta United ($70 million) and Minnesota ($100 million) followed in 2017, and Los Angeles FC hit the $100 million mark again in 2018. The record jumped to $325 million in 2022 for Charlotte and $500 million for San Diego in 2025.

In considering this impressive increase in asset value since MLS hit its tenth birthday, and particularly the past five years, the significance of this trend is only fully appreciated if the reader considers the "graveyard" of previous North American Soccer leagues.

The list is long, and the dollar amount lost was significant.

Perhaps the most famous of these failed efforts was the first edition of the NASL (North American Soccer League), which launched in 1968 and ceased operations following the 1984 season, just a decade before the United States hosted the World Cup for the first time. Like many league names (e.g., American Soccer League, United Soccer League), NASL has been used more than once.

Some credit must be given, though, to the NASL effort because its presence jump-started the conversation about soccer as a national game in the United States and Canada. Certainly, the presence of NASL must have helped in convincing FIFA to award the 1994 World Cup to the Americans.

Like many failed leagues before it, NASL's chief weaknesses (overspending on aging star players, poor owner–player relations, flawed marketing, independent owners, inconsistent club success, competition from other leagues, lack of homegrown players for fans to support, and aggressive administrative expenses) were fatal. By the time the league folded in 1985, reports suggest owners across the league were losing millions of dollars annually, and only a few clubs wanted to keep playing.

Still, NASL had some incredible highs.

At its peak, the league averaged just under fifteen thousand fans per game and had a slender television network deal. Its most famous club, the New York Cosmos, featured Pelé from 1975 to 1977, and averaged more than forty thousand spectators per game for a few seasons.

NASL's biggest win was, for the first time, achieving national media interest in the United States including coverage in leading sports publications such as *Sports Illustrated*. A reported 10 million viewers watched Pelé's inaugural NASL game and the Minnesota Kicks, a 1976 expansion club, averaged more than 32,000 fans per game in 1977.

WHY DID MLS SURVIVE AND THRIVE?

Given the precedent set by NASL's failure, how did MLS manage to survive? In fact, with losses reportedly totaling hundreds of millions of dollars overall, why did a group of owners even start again, and, against logical odds, make it work?

There are many reasons, some of which happened prior to MLS' birth, some well documented, some still developing, and others drawn from research. Future chapters will delve deeply into the points below, but the following list—in no particular order—attempts to summarize why MLS has not only survived but also, in the 2020s, thrived.

- *Demographic trends in the United States*—A glance at census statistics over the past thirty years shows a country diversifying quickly. Much of this transition has featured immigration from soccer-loving countries. The same trend has happened in Canada.

- *Pelé*—As noted earlier, arguably the greatest player of his generation but certainly the best-known global player of the time, came to play in New York City, the U.S. media capital. Although the league failed, his presence (and that of others) led to an increased, national understanding of soccer.

- *Hosting the FIFA World Cup*—The quadrennial FIFA World Cup, alongside the IOC's Olympic Games, is the most influential and far-reaching event in the world. Hosting in 1994 was a pivotal point in the game's U.S. growth. The upcoming 2026 World Cup, cohosted by the United States, Mexico, and Canada, should, by all accounts, prove equally as pivotal.

- *MLS operated as a single-entity model*—An important driver in MLS's success was a decision made at the league's launch to utilize a structure different from any other major North American professional sports league. That meant, and still means, that one organization owns the league and all its clubs. Owners of clubs are equity investors in the league, but as club operators, much like what is found with a major food chain franchise model. Each individual club has an ownership equity in the single entity and is called an "investor operator." Each new club pays an ownership fee (shown earlier in the chapter), to MLS for the right to join the league. The terms of these fees vary by club and are typically paid over several years. As noted, MLS club entry equity fees have risen more than fifty-fold since 1997.

- *The Beautiful Game*—There is no question that soccer is the world's most popular game and also the most highly participated in the United States, Canada, and Mexico. As North America becomes more and more diverse, with more people playing as kids, the relevance of the game raises MLS's value.

- *David Beckham*—there is a full chapter later in this book devoted to David Beckham's move to Los Angeles in 2007 and it firmly suggests there is no doubt his five years in MLS and the role of his celebrity partner (Victoria) played a key role. The Beckhams are crucial to the MLS success story.

- *The Soccer-specific venue*—This is referenced frequently in the book and is definitely a "key success factor" in MLS's success. Early in the league's story, leadership recognized playing in venues not suited to soccer (i.e., too big for the market demand or seating too far from the pitch) was a major obstacle. As of 2025, twenty-six of the thirty MLS clubs were playing in soccer-specific venues (typically 18,000 to 27,000 seats in terms of capacity) that were built with soccer as their primary tenant. Minnesota United FC opened Allianz Field in 2019, with 19,400 seats and a construction cost of about $200 million. Inter Miami will open its new Chase Center in 2025 with seating targeted for about 25,000. For the clubs (seven in 2025) that play in larger venues seating 35,000 to 75,000 people the MLS teams are typically there because their management also owns or has access to a venue designed for NFL, MLB, CFL, or NCAA.

- *The designated player rule*—This rule resulted from the league's investment in bringing Beckham to MLS. The decision impacted many clubs but by allowing each club to designate a player (who exceeds the salary cap), elite stars have come to MLS, without adversely impacting salary equity or a competitive balance between clubs with more resources and those with less. Some of the current group of designated players and their 2024 season salaries include Lionel Messi, Inter Miami ($20.4 million); Lorenzo Insigne, Toronto FC ($15.4 million); Xherdan Shaqiri, Chicago Fire ($8.2 million); and Sebastián Driussi, Austin FC ($6.7 million).[1]

- *Salary cap in the early days*—a common feature of most major North American sports leagues, the salary cap deters spending

1. https://www.usatoday.com/story/sports/soccer/2024/05/16/mls-salaries-lionel-messi-2024-leads-mls/73719744007/

and supports competitive balance across clubs (i.e., all clubs have a chance to win each year from a financial perspective). Although the designated player rule means MLS, similar to MLB and NBA, has more variance in payroll levels for elite players across clubs than other leagues, it still provides a controlled spending environment for most of the team. Importantly, there is an alternate view that salary caps inhibit the growth of a league, as it is more challenging to attract and retain talent. The premier leagues in Europe, for instance, do not have salary caps. The chart below, from data in a recent *USA Today* article,[2] outlines the disparity between MLS and the EPL for the top five clubs in each league. The EPL data is for the 2023–2024 season as published by football reference.[3]

Club (Europe)	2023–2024 Squad Payroll	Club (MLS)	2024 Squad Payroll
Manchester United	$261,729,552	Inter Miami	$41,700,000
Manchester City	$255,720,441	Toronto FC	$31,400,000
Arsenal	$211,204,180	Chicago Fire	$23,100,000
Chelsea	$274,340,278	Nashville SC	$21,400,000
Liverpool	$173,302,521	FC Cincinnati	$18,700,000

As noted in the table, the salaries differ considerably, including the minimum salary, which is $89,716 for MLS[4] and, although not specifically reported, a number of $10,000 per week (or about $400,000 for an August to May season) is shared in a number of reports as the lowest pay for EPL players in England.

- *Global sponsors*—MLS clubs are of high interest to sponsors, particularly jersey sponsors, who are targeting global audiences and not just North Americans.

---

2. https://www.usatoday.com/story/sports/soccer/2024/05/16/mls-salaries-lionel-messi-2024-leads-mls/73719744007/
3. https://fbref.com/en/comps/9/wages/Premier-League-Wages
4. https://www.mlssoccer.com/about/roster-rules-and-regulations

- *Lionel Messi*—Although this part of the story is still developing, the signing of one of the greatest players ever, coming off his historic FIFA 2022 World Cup win, validated MLS's upside and potential for continued growth.

EXPERT PERSPECTIVE: MURALEE DAS, FORMER ASSISTANT GENERAL SECRETARY, ASIAN FOOTBALL CONFEDERATION

The North American soccer market and the Asian Football Confederation (AFC), where I worked for many years as their assistant general secretary, shared the problem of professional leagues that were not sustainable and were long shots. Multiple leagues were launched; most existed on life support and then were eventually buried. The story of MLS and other new Asian professional soccer leagues, however, are ones about bold start-ups, private equity investment, and multiple twists.

When FIFA awarded the United States the 1994 World Cup, there were no real pro soccer leagues in North America. MLS kicked off only in 1996, without a CBA, and promptly got sued by their own players for antitrust practices. I remember reading the appeal court judgment in 2002 while at the AFC, and saw the appeal judge finally dismissed the players' claim because he felt they could play at other leagues elsewhere (in short, MLS was not an effective monopoly). MLS literally survived because of that one court decision after six years of litigation.

It was a bold gamble on a startup league by early investors like Phil Anschutz and Lamar Hunt, and they won the bet.

At the same time as MLS's early dicey future, across the Pacific Ocean, I was part of one of the world's biggest soccer experiments that few have heard about. Unlike MLS, no one wanted to invest in Asian leagues. Asian billionaires were more inclined to own Manchester City, Queens Park Rangers, or Leicester City.

In 2002, the AFC's leagues faced the same predicament as MLS. Few high-quality international players wanted to play in

Asian leagues, most leagues were burning cash, and very few Asian players had reached the pinnacle of playing in the European leagues.

Asian broadcasters were keener to buy the rights to telecast matches of visiting English Premier League clubs like Manchester United. In the face of those realities, the AFC decided to use private equity funding. Why didn't the AFC "acquire" those leagues from their national associations, transform them, and then "sell" them back to their owners at zero cost?

The end game was to increase the collective value of all Asian soccer properties and then attract viewership, fan interest, and investors. It was a moonshot moment, and one that made the executives at FIFA wary. At its core it was about the AFC "acquiring" about thirty professional football leagues across Asia. Yes, thirty!

The AFC called the strategy "Vision Asia." Launched in 2002, it was designed to create wholesale changes from how football associations were managed, how leagues were run, how grassroot programs were changed, coaching credentials upgraded, and making largely amateur clubs and associations into professional organizations.

The AFC president tasked me to globally recruit, in about twelve months, one hundred of the best tactical soccer minds in order to make Vision Asia a reality. It was the single largest recruitment exercise of that scale in the sports industry—ever.

In that one year, I was constantly on the phone interviewing hundreds, meeting potential recruits every day from all six continents, headhunting, and then making employment offers that changed many lives and ours. We flew these new professionals (we called them consultants) all over Asia, and "took over" many leagues. In just seven incredible years, as the AFC transformed these leagues and clubs, Vision Asia became a massive commercial success. The AFC rights agreement, worth about $80 million in 2002, skyrocketed to become about US$1 billion in 2009. It was our 10x moment. We also won our gamble.

At the AFC, we studied the MLS story closely.

In fact, I tried to recruit MLS executives from their marketing company, Soccer United Marketing. I had spent time in America, completing university, and knew American entrepreneurship was unparalleled. We needed the start-up mindset at AFC, as our "private equity" strategy was taking shape. We eventually hired the first Americans to ever work in the Asian soccer governing body.

Our first American recruit was the director of communication who came from Los Angeles. Years later after leaving the AFC, while consulting, I kept in touch with American soccer executives. It was clear to me MLS recognized that to thrive, they had to leverage three competitive advantages that no other major soccer league possessed—their single entity league ownership structure, the American immigrant dream, and artificial intelligence (AI) superiority.

The MLS CBA attracted and allowed relatively low-paid talent to come to America, because these players wanted to live the American dream and eventually reside in the United States. In 2019, astonishingly, MLS held the third highest proportion (56 percent) of foreign players for a major soccer league.

When this foreign talent arrived, MLS used AI to significantly improve the quality of their play, and collectively the quality of the league. The United States is a technological hub, and MLS teams partnered with multiple AI companies, about ten years before the current AI wave of excitement.

Other top soccer leagues in England, Germany, and France were laggards in using AI because they were already magnets for great talent (due to higher compensation, of course), and that reality probably didn't justify an investment in AI.

Even back in 2015, about fifteen MLS teams were already using global positioning system technology, player tracking data sensors, stadium-wide sensors, web platforms, and other AI systems. It helped that other American sports like basketball were also heavily investing in AI, and the use of AI in sports had been normalized in U.S. sports. The quality of play dramatically improved for MLS.

About ten years later, MLS's and AFC's ascendency as leagues changed.

While the AFC eventually exited and "sold" those leagues back to the national associations mostly around 2011 (when there was a leadership change at AFC), very few of the newly independent soccer leagues in Asia invested in technology (unlike MLS).

Without a focused private equity strategy, and now with multiple owners of leagues (compared to a single "owner" like MLS), only a handful of Asian leagues thrived such as Japan, South Korea, Australia, Saudi Arabia, and Qatar.

In contrast, MLS has used their three competitive advantages extremely well over the years. MLS's US$2.5 billion streaming broadcast deal with Apple alone is probably worth more than the AFC's entire continental streaming value.

People often forget all this strategizing for MLS did not take place accidentally, and for that Sunil Gulati (U.S. Soccer president, 2006–2018) and Don Garber, MLS's long-serving MLS commissioner, should be credited as the leaders and architects of the MLS revolution.

The impact of their leadership over the past twenty-five years is evident and clearly the most successful start-up investment in modern sports business. I know, because I was there, working in world football, watching MLS, all while contributing to the professionalization of Asian soccer leagues.

I also witnessed firsthand at the AFC how it felt to take bold gambles to change the competitiveness in sports. Soccer and many of its team and clubs today are innovative start-ups and even private equity play, but so few people outside the game recognize and understand the kind of governance innovation and risk at FIFA, AFC, U.S. Soccer, and MLS to make these leagues some of the world's biggest.

I have been a Major League Soccer fan since the opening whistle being blown on April 6, 1996. I excitedly tuned into ESPN's coverage of the inaugural MLS match and watched a late Eric Wynalda goal secure all three points for San Jose Clash against a D.C. United team led by former NCAA college coaches Bruce Arena and his assistant Bob Bradley.

I had a very brief flirtation with the league during the early stages of 1996 when I was completing my senior year at Hartwick College in Upstate New York. After classes on a cold, wintry February day I returned to my dorm room to a flashing light on my answering machine. I eagerly listened to an animated message from a Hartwick alum congratulating me on being selected in the MLS Inaugural Player Draft. There was no social media or around the clock news updates on MLS draft day back in 1996. Thankfully my isolation in Oneonta, New York, prohibited me from sharing this breaking news with my friends and family. It did, however, take several hours for me to clarify that I was not in fact a new employee of our fledgling professional soccer league. It was Canadian international and former Hartwick College sweeper Iain Fraser who had been selected by New England Revolution with the fifth overall pick.

That was as close as I ever got to being in the league—one beautiful afternoon of misguided hope as I dared to dream.

On March 4, 1996, three additional rounds of the MLS college draft would come and go without my name appearing. But college stars such as Eddie Pope, Greg Vanney, Jesse Marsch, Miles Joseph, Steve Ralston, Ante Razov, and Eddie Lewis would start their own professional careers here in the United States. Major League Soccer had officially arrived.

College soccer has played, and will continue to play, an important role in the development and continued success of MLS. The league has certainly experienced highs and lows after a successful 1994 World Cup here in the United States provided a tremendous opportunity. The college soccer ecosystem has always supported the league, been a good teammate, and cheered loudly from the sidelines.

The SuperDraft has clearly diminished in significance through the years. The dependency on college players shouldering the heavy lifting on the pitch has been replaced with designated players, increased sponsorship revenue, and an influx of international talent. MLS teams, however, continue to see value in drafting the right college players to complement their established stars. I have proudly watched in recent years as our own Syracuse University players such as Miles Robinson, Kamal Miller, Alex Bono, Tajon Buchanan, Ryan Raposo, Deandre Kerr, and Levonte Johnson have successfully transitioned into MLS. There is still no better feeling than hearing the name of a Syracuse University player called during MLS draft day. It sends chills down your spine, and you are excited (and nervous with anticipation) as each young man embarks upon the next step of their soccer journey and transitions into the professional ranks.

Important decisions being made on the pitch, on the sidelines, and within the front offices of our beloved MLS clubs continue to be influenced by individuals who started their physical and intellectual football journeys on college campuses across our country. The front office and the technical staff of each MLS team are often filled with talent developed through the college game. Twelve of the twenty-nine current managers in MLS came through the college soccer system. Historically, the impact of coaches such as Sigi Schmid, Bruce Arena, Bob Bradley, and Greg Berhalter upon both our domestic and international game has been remarkable. There is a complexity to MLS that can benefit from individuals who are familiar with the league and our unique soccer landscape here in the United States.

The relationship between MLS and college soccer continues to be refined and evolves each year. But there is a shared passion, a love, and a commitment to ensuring that our professional soccer league succeeds and grows. We are partners. We are teammates. We have both been entrusted with the responsibility of carefully passing on this beautiful game to the next generation of players and fans as we welcome the 2026 World Cup back to our shores.

CHAPTER FIVE

How the 1994 FIFA World Cup Shaped MLS

On July 4, 1988, the United States was selected to host the 1994 FIFA World Cup.

At the time, soccer was not what it is today in the United States. It was still on the fringes of mainstream sport with no coverage on ESPN SportsCenter. Only a small percentage of Americans could name any top global players.

It was a summer sport for young Canadian hockey players, and in America, while U8 participation rates were growing, soccer seemed to lag well behind tryouts for football, basketball, lacrosse, or baseball/softball teams.

For immigrants to North America, many who brought a passion for soccer with them, getting up early on Saturday mornings to watch European games was far more common than following any North American league or team. For these individuals, their fan affinity was 100 percent focused on where they came from, not where they were.

These weren't glory days for the sport in North America, but the sport's leaders were determined to challenge that.

When FIFA awarded the 1994 Cup to the United States, many who follow the sport closely were dismayed. The other leading candidates to host the 1994 World Cup were Brazil (a traditional soccer hotbed) and Morocco (another country where soccer is the most popular sport). Of note, Morocco will co-host, with Spain and Portugal, the 2030 FIFA World Cup.

The awarding of the fifteenth edition of this major event—the 1994 FIFA World Cup—led to accusations of "bias" and "commercialization." However, most public reports and the rationale put forward by many FIFA representatives for the decision was based on the efficiency of the U.S. bid (where every stadium was already built) combined with operational flaws in the Brazil and Moroccan bids.

North American fans were—for the most part—interested, but globally, many questioned the decision, which would send twenty-three national teams plus the United States to vie for the world's greatest team sport trophy.

The World Cup tournament itself, held in June and July 1994, produced much success. Brazil was crowned champion, the fourth time they had captured the Cup. Attendance records were set with more than 3.5 million entering nine different U.S. venues, an average of just under 69,000 per game (the previous high was just more than 50,000 per game for the 1966 World Cup).

The event also produced further milestones.

Notably, it saw the first participation of a unified German team (West Germany was the defending champion) since before World War II, and the first World Cup game played indoors on temporary, transplanted natural grass in Detroit's domed stadium (the Pontiac Silverdome). The 1994 World Cup also marked the first time Saudi Arabia, now a major player in hosting or influencing world sport, qualified.

Several prominent soccer nations did not qualify for the 1994 World Cup, including France, four United Kingdom nations (England, Northern Ireland, Scotland, and Wales), plus Denmark (winners of the 1992 European championship), Portugal, Japan, and Uruguay.

Argentine legend and the star of the 1986 World Cup, Diego Maradona, started the 1994 World Cup, his fourth, but was sent home after failing a drug test (for a weight-loss drug) after scoring a goal and assisting on two others in Argentina's first two games, both wins. The team struggled after his departure, losing their next two games.

Two goal-scoring records that remain today were also set in 1994. Both came during the same game. First, Cameroon's legend, Roger Milla, became, at forty-two, the oldest scorer of a World Cup goal. Second, one player scoring five goals in a single game happened when Oleg Salenko led Russia to a 6–1 win over Milla's Cameroon.

Looking back at the 1994 World Cup, which the FIFA Museum notes "is considered one of the most successful sporting events worldwide," makes clear that 1994 was a pivotal point in soccer's North American ascendancy. This attendance record stood as one key indicator, but it was so much more than that. The Cup put the United States on the soccer map.

The December 1993 draw, held in Las Vegas before a live audience, was broadcast nationally on ESPN in the United States and Eurosport and is estimated to have reached millions worldwide. Of note, although the assignment of teams to groups was done randomly, the organizing committee then assigned—the Eurosport commentator used the word "manipulated"—the locations of the groups to the nine host cities. Many assumed this was to aid in ticket sales.

For instance, the Italian and Irish teams were based in New York City, home to large Italian and Irish populations and Manhattan's famed "Little Italy" district.

The 1994 World Cup also included some important rule changes to help increase scoring at the World Cup. A win was now worth three points in group play, versus the previous two, to better incentivize winning a game versus playing for a one-point draw. Another rule change that was used at the World Cup for the first time in 1994, after being based in 1992, prevented goalkeepers from picking up the ball if a teammate passed it back to them.

Finally, following the low-scoring 1990 World Cup in Italy, FIFA changed the rule for offsides to now allow an attacking player to be onside if they were in line with the final defensive player, as opposed to having to always have a defensive player between the offensive striker and the goaltender. The above changes were intended to optimize offense and scoring.

On the marketing front, in addition to strategically selecting key markets for group play, the organizers—for the first time in the broadcasting of soccer in the United States—went to commercial-free coverage of all the matches of the World Cup, meaning every minute of action was telecast (unlike prior coverage).

In taking a page from the sport of ice hockey, and the NHL, the 1994 World Cup introduced player names on the back of their jerseys. This was known, from the NHL, to assist player recognition, merchandise sales, and player branding.

Interestingly, there were other changes suggested by FIFA to increase marketability leading into the 1994 World Cup, including a report that FIFA considered moving from two forty-five-minute halves to four twenty-five-minute quarters to generate more commercial breaks for television. This change did not happen.

Many of those decisions that were enacted for 1994 appeared to work.

First, the number of goals scored per game went from 2.2 at the 1990 World Cup up to 2.8 at the 1994 World Cup. Second, a 1994 *Sports Illustrated* article indicated the 1994 FIFA World Cup attracted 32 billion cumulative television viewers, including 2 billion for the Italy-Brazil final, where Brazil won on penalty kicks (despite finishing third in their group and sneaking in as one of the better third-place teams).

One of the highlights of the entire tournament was Italy's first-round 1–0 loss at Giants Stadium in New Jersey, an upset win by the Republic of Ireland in a sold-out venue (75,338) that was raucous from the start and clearly pro-Irish.

That same *Sports Illustrated* article estimated a total economic impact for the United States of $4 billion from hosting the tournament, outlining the massive tourism, and investment dollars that foreign visitors brought to America.

THE LEGACY OF THE 1994 WORLD CUP

The 1994 FIFA World Cup was held in nine U.S. cities more than three decades ago. Yes, thirty-one years, or nearly two generations ago. The world population has increased by more than two and a half billion people since then. The U.S. population has grown by more than 80 million and technology has advanced to a level few could have imagined. Sports have evolved considerably.

It is a different world today than it was in 1994.

The same can be said for soccer. Many argue that hosting the 1994 World Cup set the stage for the debut and sustained existence of MLS, the first major television rights deals for the sport in the United States (e.g., Fox and the English Premier League, ESPN and the UEFA Champions League).

Perhaps the best way to summarize the impact of the 1994 World Cup is with the return of the World Cup to North America in 2026. With intense anticipation and an expanded continental hosting structure, with Mexico and Canada joining the United States, most expect the event to exceed the 1994 World Cup in its impact on soccer. The footprint of the World Cup will be much bigger. Three countries hosting, not one. The number of countries participating doubled to forty-eight. The total number of games will also double, from 52 to 104. A total of sixteen major cities will host games, up from nine. This includes Atlanta, Boston, Dallas, Guadalajara, Houston, Kansas City, Los Angeles, Mexico City, Miami, Monterrey, New York/New Jersey, Philadelphia, San Francisco, Seattle, Toronto, and Vancouver. Many cities not on that list were left disappointed following the selection process. The final will be held in the New York City area.

An Insider's View of the 1994 World Cup

The 1994 FIFA World Cup was held in multiple U.S. cities during the time when I worked as a protocol manager on the San Francisco venue management team. I dealt with all the VIPs, ticketing, and hospitality requests. Peter Bridgewater was my boss/mentor and a legend in U.S. soccer. A former Manchester policeman with a disciplined management style, he was one of the founding fathers of the NASL.

He also owned the first iteration of the San Jose Earthquakes and brought me on to the team since we had worked together previously when I was a marketing manager at the Oakland Coliseum hosting Mexican national team friendlies.

At the San Francisco venue, six matches were held at Stanford University, including some great matches. The US–Brazil quarterfinal on the Fourth of July was one of these and could not have been scripted better. Brazil's team, which would ultimately win the 1994 World Cup, was headquartered right near our venue and played a few games there. Looking back, it seems like it was a nonstop party for a month.

That said, at the time the stadium was a dump. Lots of seats, but no seatbacks, with many of the rows really not in good shape. There were no suites in the venue. We had all these dignitaries coming in (country presidents, movie stars, etc.) and needed to create a makeshift VIP area. We used tents for that.

They had a tent outside of the stadium for food service. It was not anywhere near what you'd see today or what was available in Europe at the time. When FIFA and the host committee picked the venue, they thought about various spots knowing the Bay Area was a soccer hotbed. There were also no other options. The Giants' and A's stadiums were off-limits due to the presence of a very real baseball season.

After the 1994 World Cup, I really caught the soccer bug and realized the excellence and the incredible athleticism of the Brazilian team. It was eye-opening because prior to that amazing tournament, I was not a serious fan.

Today, the 1994 World Cup is viewed as the springboard that was needed to get potential investors and media partners onside for a domestic league. The success the 1994 World Cup organizers had in selling tickets, sponsorship, generating TV ratings, and achieving overall profitability was the key to getting MLS up and running.

Of course, Alan Rothenberg, who ran the 1994 World Cup, was the man who segued the management team from the 1994 World Cup to set the stage for MLS and its success. The early investors included the Hunts, Anschutzs, Krafts, and others, who were brought in by Rothenberg. He was the reason they came to the party.

When you ask why the 1994 World Cup was so transformational for soccer, I think the world was getting smaller and the rise of the internet and digital media was coming, so the global connectivity was there. Further, the United States was sort of an island that had been resistant to soccer. The Americans got exposed to the game and saw that it was more than something for little kids to play on the weekend. The 1994 Cup proved soccer could generate fan interest.

My impression is that much of the success of the 1994 World Cup was linked to the success of the 1984 Olympic Games in Los Angeles. Rothenberg was involved in both. And the big commercial brands that made the LA Games work could also be linked to the 1994 World Cup. My sense is that the global brands knew how big this World Cup was going to be and wanted to be part of it. Alan and his team were able to sign those sponsors and then delivered a spectacular return on investment.

In every respect, the World Cup overdelivered. This was vital to the success of MLS. If the World Cup had been a money loser or had featured empty stadiums, I doubt the league would have even launched.

What stands out thirty years later is the longer-term vision that surrounded that World Cup. Soccer wasn't going to fade into the past. Instead, because of the strategic initiatives taken by a group of talented people, a whole new framework was built for soccer in America.

If 1994 hadn't worked, we would not have gotten the Women's World Cup in 1999. And while the payoff for the women was not immediate, the NWSL is well on its way to emulating MLS's success.

Going back to 1994, there was this longer-term vision that was key to setting the stage for a successful league with the business opportunities as a whole for the entire MLS community that was part of it. Not surprisingly, the big three families—Kraft, Anschutz, and Hunt—kept investing. It made all the difference.

*Major League Soccer: From the Wiz to Credibility in Less Than
Three Decades*

It was a bit underwhelming at the start.

Following the hosting of one of the most successful World Cups
of all time (FIFA's 1994 World Cup), the United States was ready
to unveil its first ten teams in a new professional soccer league at
the New York Palladium on October 17, 1995.

Yet entering the Palladium that afternoon, it felt less like a
transformative moment and more like a small group of dedicated
soccer fans were going to give one more try to make the sport stick
in the United States.

The road ahead looked daunting. Leagues had tried before—
and even Pelé had not been able to make it work in North America.
We had basketball, baseball, ice hockey, and the other football. Was
there room for another major sport? They were going to try. This
time it would be major—Major League Soccer to be precise.

As the teams were announced, the nervousness increased.
Were we really going to get excited about the Wiz and the Revolution, the Mutiny, the Clash? These were not traditional soccer
names, and the uniforms didn't alleviate the concern. Bright colors
with flashy logos. Honestly, only D.C. United looked like a soccer
club; the rest were too cartoonish for my palette.

I promised to remain committed to this great experiment—but
even the most loyal had to wonder if this league would have legs.

Playing on football fields with the gridiron markings clearly
visible, it was often difficult to follow where the touchlines were on
TV. There was one other thing. MLS teams were junior tenants in
other people's playgrounds.

By the year 2000 (five years in) it was reported the league had
lost over $250 million, and by 2002 it still stood at ten teams (with
some expansion and contraction)—but even more worrying was

that there were just three owners—and one of them, Phil Anschutz, owned six teams. Could you even imagine an NFL where one individual owned six franchises? That's right, you couldn't.

It was simple and decisions needed to be made. The league needed to stabilize or shut down. Surely, Anschutz, Lamar Hunt, and Robert Kraft (the three owners) weren't going to continue taking a collective bath.

MLS needed at least three things: expansion to other markets, diversified ownership, and the creation of soccer-specific stadiums. But more than anything it needed additional time—minutes, hours, days, months, years, and decades—to improve the talent and credibility, and attract a much bigger, scalable audience.

In 1999, the Columbus Crew decided to build the first soccer-specific stadium. It was a game-changer. Nothing sapped enthusiasm more than seeing a soccer fan sitting with 15,000 other people in a 60,000-person football stadium.

With Columbus, fans could sit in *their* arena and support *their* team.

In that same period, Garber sat with leadership in a meeting that was supposed to focus on cost cutting and maybe contracting the league.[1] Instead, Garber doubled down and asked for more money and more commitment—especially to build a product that would create a national TV audience. I wasn't there—so I am guilty of spreading stories—but many say that meeting saved and repositioned the league.

Slowly more teams were added, and more owners came on board. The league was even charging a franchise fee. Can you believe it? The league was losing money and asking wealthy investors to pay for a franchise *and* build a new stadium for their team.

---

1. https://www.wsj.com/articles/SB115051121239083200

On the one hand, I get it. There are only so many people who can say they own a sports franchise in the United States. They're not offering expansion NFL and NBA teams much these days—and the price of entry is incredibly high.

But for the price of adding a franchise in say, Salt Lake City in 2004, you might have considered buying an existing team (with a stadium and a fan base) in the Premier League (England) or Ligue 1 (France).

With the proliferation of sports on TV came both an opportunity and a threat. An initial contract with ESPN/ABC and Univision in 2006 did create stability in revenue, but the ratings were poor, and many matches expected to be on ABC were moved to ESPN.

Then, in 2013, NBC announced a significant investment in the English Premier League. MLS had consistently been challenged by the fact that it was the third most popular soccer league in the United States (behind Liga MX and the Premier League).

It would be like having American basketball fans tell friends they would rather watch German or Canadian basketball than the NBA.

Once again, MLS showed its resilience and announced a significant, long-term contract with ESPN, Fox, and Univision.

Feeding off each other was the stability of the new TV contract with the consistent expansion of the league and the commitment to purpose-built stadiums. FC Cincinnati and Nashville agreed to pay $150 million franchise fees in 2019 and create stadiums soon. Austin soon followed—and these mid-markets (ranked by size between twenty-sixth—Cincinnati and forty-fifth—Nashville) meant soccer became a large part of the social fabric of their towns. Soccer became the cool ticket, and the experience didn't disappoint—with rowdy "ultras," constant chanting, and great hospitality.

While the league was growing in mid-markets it was also creating stability in the major media markets—critical to the growth of the TV audience. New York City FC joined in 2015, Atlanta joined in 2017, and LAFC became the second LA team in 2018.

These new clubs seemed generations away from that first day at the Palladium. MLS has expanded from ten to twenty-nine teams (with the thirtieth on the books for 2025). The teams look more legit (even the Wiz decided to change to Sporting Kansas City and dialed down the uniforms), the ownership is considerably more stable, and the product is significantly better.

If the first five years of the league represented MLS 1.0, then 2.0 started in 2000 and is finally ending. Now comes MLS 3.0—and what will make this era so interesting is it is built around the event that started it all—the World Cup. If the 1994 World Cup was the stimulus for the league to start—what will the 2026 World Cup bring?

I think there are four things to look at in MLS 3.0.

First is the growth of the unique, ten-year media partnership with Apple TV. Instantly, people anywhere in the world can watch every MLS match live. No other league can say that. Will this become the platform for global growth?

Second, MLS is strategically building an alliance with the Mexican League Liga MX. Remember—Liga MX has more fans in the United States than MLS. This partnership is currently the creation of a Cup tournament between the two leagues. In the future, I see even greater synergies especially around player movement (both ways).

Speaking of players, I believe the third trend is the further development of world-class MLS academies, training facilities, and the development of talent. The soccer talent is here, what has been missing is the path from junior to the pros. There are examples such as MLS Next, MLS's youth elite league with more than fifteen thousand players. This may not be a popular opinion, but I contend that within ten years no one from MLS will have played college soccer. All the talent will come from foreign leagues or will be homegrown at club-owned academies. Like Europe, you will see youth players committing to franchises at thirteen and fourteen years old and breaking into first-division teams as early as sixteen and seventeen.

Last but not least is the coming FIFA World Cup 2026. Not only will the United States, Mexico, and Canada put on a great event (as the U.S. did in 1994) but this time the Americans (who will host the final game) will be doing it as a legitimate soccer nation. I believe the world will be watching and duly impressed.

I was truly fortunate to be involved in FIFA's World Cup 1994. For those of us fanatical about soccer, it was the opportunity to work on a global event—but do it in our own backyard. The people I worked with were dedicated and committed to both the tournament and the growth of the sport in this country.

It was a fascinating journey, and I would be lying if I told you I knew it would work. I was skeptical. Without the dedication and commitment of people like Don Garber, Phil Anschutz, Robert Kraft, and the Hunt family I am convinced it wouldn't have happened.

In 2025, the thirtieth team joined the league—with San Diego reportedly paying a $500 million franchise fee. In 1996 that would have seemed laughable. I don't think there's a league in any sport anywhere in the world that can point to so much growth in such a short period of time.

I'm just glad I've been around to watch these beautiful moments.

Chapter Six

MLS and David Beckham

Why an Englishman's Arrival Tipped the Scales

IF SOMEONE LIVES ON PLANET EARTH, IS MORE THAN TWENTY YEARS old, and has paid even scant attention to soccer media coverage, they know the David Beckham story. He is a household name in North America, Europe, Asia, South America, Africa, and Australia. So much so that the 2023 blockbuster Netflix series *Beckham* celebrated his global storybook tale.

As a child, he dreamed of playing for Manchester United, which he ultimately did from 1995 to 2003 (although he had started with United's juniors in 1991 and was "loaned" to Preston North End for the 1994–1995 season). During that span, Beckham won numerous accolades and championships. He also played for legendary European clubs Paris Saint-Germain, Real Madrid, AC Milan, and, in MLS, the LA Galaxy.

His model-like good looks and fashion-conscious style made him a sex symbol for many. He married—and remains married to—a Spice Girl. In 2015, *People* magazine named him the sexiest man alive. On top of all that, he:

- Represented his country on the world's biggest stages, although never captured a major championship for England. Still, his passion, stories, and fan following remain legendary.
- Showed an ability to kick the ball and "bend it," which led to famous goals, highly watched replays, a feeling he could score or

set up a goal from anywhere on the pitch, and then had a popular movie named after him (2002's *Bend It Like Beckham*). In many circles, Beckham is best known for scoring more than two-thirds of his goals from a set position (i.e., free, corner, or penalty kick).

- Scored, and continues to secure, endorsement deals with the world's biggest (and hippest) brands including Armani, adidas, Gillette, Motorola, Pepsi, and H&M.

- Supported the fashion empire his wife, Victoria Beckham, built.

- Built the Beckham "brand," long considered one of the strongest athlete brands in history, and one that has successfully continued during his athletic retirement.

- Played more than 500 professional games, scoring 97 goals, and setting up 152 more. For his country, England, he won 115 caps and scored 17 goals in those 115 matches, including three World Cups (1998, 2002, 2006).

- Enjoyed having *Forbes* magazine name him 2008's fifth most powerful celebrity in the world.

The above bullet points are a long way of suggesting Beckham's trophy case is full. He won titles in England, France, Italy, the United States, and Spain. The list is impressive: six English Premier League titles, two FA Cups, four Community Shields, a Champions League title, two MLS Cups, a single Ligue 1 title, and the La Liga championship.

In retirement, he has become a club owner and his presence in the game remains clear. He was a dedicated and gifted athlete who became a charismatic and attractive celebrity.

Beckham is also a shrewd businessperson who created an extraordinary impact on MLS, first as a player and then as an owner.

WHERE DID DAVID BECKHAM COME FROM?
Beckham was identified as a phenom from virtually the moment he first touched a soccer ball. As early as eleven years of age, he gained recognition and won local skills competitions.

His talent and athletic prowess were quickly evident and due to his exceptional kicking and passing abilities from a distance, he played midfield most of his career. Signing his first professional contract at sixteen, he ultimately played at the highest levels of the sport before he turned twenty. Fans, money, celebrity, and opportunity came his way thereafter.

Beckham reportedly came from a strong and supportive family, growing up with two sisters. His parents were working class Londoners. His dad repaired appliances and his mother styled hair. They were Manchester United fans.

Today, Beckham is a father of four and has been married for more than twenty-five years, a rarity for international celebrities. In addition, in 2024, the *Sunday Times* Rich List estimated the Beckhams' (David and wife Victoria) wealth at $577 million.

Beckham's public image, with some negative media coverage thrown in, has consistently shown him to be a family man, savvy business operator, long-term husband, and frequent philanthropist supporting charities such as UNICEF as an ambassador for UNICEF's Unite Against AIDS Campaign.

BECKHAM AND MLS

Although Beckham did not make his debut with the LA Galaxy until late in July 2007, the announcement of his coming to MLS was made in early 2007 when he officially signed on January 11. The Galaxy sold more than five thousand season tickets during the two days following and the Beckham experiment was "on."

Of course, Beckham wasn't the first major global star to sign on to play soccer in the United States, but he was the first of his level (i.e., one of the top few players on the planet) to select MLS. True, luminaries like Pelé and Gerd Müller had joined the NASL, a pre-MLS league, in the 1970s, but Beckham was the first big name to endorse MLS, and *Sports Illustrated* thought as much when it featured him on the July 16, 2007 cover asking, "Will He Change the Fate of American Soccer?"

Beckham's signing also led to other global superstars coming to MLS, including luminaries such as Thierry Henry (NY Red Bulls), Zlatan Ibrahimović (LA Galaxy), Lorenzo Insigne (Toronto FC), Wayne

Rooney (D.C. United), Frank Lampard and David Villa (New York City FC), and most recently Lionel Messi (Inter Miami FC). In most cases, the players came in their thirties following long careers in Europe's premier leagues. Some had notable on-field success—especially Henry and Ibrahimović—while others were competent but not startling. Some returned to Europe to play again before retiring and others took on coaching and/or ownership roles post-retirement.

Beckham started it all. Even today, the "Beckham effect" on MLS remains considerable.

It is perhaps much like the impact Wayne Gretzky, arguably the greatest ice hockey player of all time, had on ice hockey, when he moved to the Los Angeles Kings in 1988. It was a transformational, bumpy move that took time, but the result was an elevation of hockey and the NHL in the United States. Ironically, it also focused on a Los Angeles–based franchise.

At the time of the announcement, Beckham was not just the best-known soccer player in the world, but also one of the best-known celebrities regardless of industry. He was at the level of Michael Jordan, Tiger Woods, and Roger Federer.

Admittedly, he was over thirty, but barely thirty-one, and still very much in his prime. His decision was seen as a big deal and immediately captured global attention.

In the seven months of anticipation that followed, as Beckham completed his season with Real Madrid, the legendary La Liga club that won the league championship that season, the media attention, expectation, pressure, criticism, and chatter was feverish—particularly in England, Beckham's home country.

Public responses ranged from flabbergasted to anger to excitement to folly. At the time, and to a lesser extent since, the level of play of MLS was viewed as well below that of the top European leagues. Many felt Beckham was too good for MLS.

Finally, July came.

Beckham suited up for the LA Galaxy in a friendly against Chelsea that July, followed by his MLS debut in August. He made an impact in the first two games he started, scoring a goal and adding three assists, but a knee injury limited his playing time for the rest of the 2007 season.

Many of those who thought Beckham's decision was folly, or found themselves flabbergasted at the news of his signing, cited the massive pay cut he was taking from his $20 million annual salary in La Liga to a measly $6.5 million for the Galaxy.

Few at the time knew the details of his contract (it was not shared publicly), which meant he was about to become the highest-paid player in the world, with numerous other benefits that would accrue over time. They also underestimated his ability to help catalyze the growth and development of MLS and turn the league into a major, sustainable, and established entity.

This is where Simon Fuller enters the discussion. Fuller, Beckham's longtime agent from 2003 to 2019, is given credit, including by Beckham, for his LA Galaxy contract and much of the creation of "Brand Beckham" with its impact touching endorsements, sponsorship, retail presence, merchandise items, fashion, new businesses, media, production, and more.

A quick look into Fuller's background shows he was much more than an agent to Beckham. Fuller worked with the Spice Girls, including Beckham's wife Victoria, Andy Murray, Carrie Underwood, ABBA, Lewis Hamilton, Madonna, Kelly Clarkson, and Annie Lennox, among many other A-list entertainers.

He is a philanthropist, investor, entrepreneur, and perhaps best known as a television producer of shows like *Pop Idol*, *American Idol*, and *So You Think You Can Dance*. His accolades include recognition on the Hollywood Walk of Fame.

The contract that Beckham and Fuller worked out with the LA Galaxy and MLS included a base salary of $6.5 million annually to play for five years with the Galaxy. As noted, that amount was only about a third of his previous pay from Real Madrid. But the contract included two key benefits as follows:

1. The option to purchase an MLS expansion club after retirement for $25 million.

2. Additional pay based on a percentage of LA Galaxy club revenues (i.e., sponsorship, merchandise, media, tickets).

An additional benefit, not related to soccer, was providing Victoria Beckham the opportunity to move to Los Angeles, which most reports suggest helped her various entertainment initiatives.

For Beckham, the move resulted in very positive outcomes (a "win-win") for MLS and for the Beckhams. In the first case, although expansion fees in the MLS were about $10 million in 2007, they have skyrocketed since to $500 million in 2025. The asset appreciation on his Inter Miami franchise is considerable.

Second, reports suggest his move resulted in league-wide revenues that led to an annual income for Beckham of more than $50 million. This made him the highest-paid athlete in the world at the time.

What follows here is a short compilation of evidence to support Beckham's influence on MLS between 2007 and 2025.

1. The league has gone from thirteen to thirty clubs, including Beckham's partial ownership of Inter Miami. This means the number of jobs for MLS players went from about three hundred to nearly nine hundred and generated much happiness among professional soccer players. The average salary has also gone up nearly five times, to more than $500,000 per player in 2025.

2. Average attendance has jumped from about 16,000 to 23,234 in 2024. That has made owners and investors happy.

3. Expansion fees for a new franchise from the $10 million that Toronto FC paid to join in 2007 to the reported $500 million for San Diego FC to join for the 2025 season. More happiness for owners.

4. Media rights have gone from less than $10 million annually to an estimated $250 million per year, thanks to the stunning Apple contract.

5. According to *Sportico* and *Forbes*, the average MLS club in 2024 is worth $678 million. This is up from $37 million in 2008.

These are just five data points illustrating Beckham's impact on MLS. There are others.

Beckham, himself, certainly came out on top. In addition to his rev-share-driven salary in his five MLS seasons with the Galaxy, his option for an expansion club at $25 million worked out quite well.

In its 2024 valuations, *Sportico* estimated Inter Miami to be worth $1.02 billion. This is more than forty times the expansion fee paid. Based on a 2007 valuation, it is just 5 percent of what the owners of San Diego FC reportedly paid ($500 million) for their new franchise, which debuted in 2025.

Looking back, eighteen years after his decision to join MLS, the effects are clear, extensive, and border on the extraordinary. On one hand, it's easy to argue the time was finally right to sign a player of Beckham's stature. On the other hand, though, MLS and its owners and commissioner deserve a huge amount of credit for taking this risk.

There is one other thing. The Beckham contract also required MLS and its owners and commissioner—the "other side of the table"—to agree to take the risk on him, forgo a percentage of revenues, and risk franchise asset valuations by committing to another expansion team of unknown location and status.

Although any public record of these discussions and this side of the famous contract do not exist, we can assume, or at least infer, that leading up to the 2007 contract and announcement, MLS must have constructed deep analysis, held numerous strategic discussions, and offered up forward-thinking risk assessments.

They should get the same credit for business acumen and foresight Beckham and Fuller widely receive. MLS's leadership and ownership group took a massive chance but benefited enormously.

Beckham did as well, forgoing prime earning years in La Liga (or another premier league), but not to the same level of benefit as MLS owners, whose thinking would've considered and factored in the list of failed franchises from the NASL. Where there are failed leagues, there are significant investment losses. Some difficult discussions took place.

Why Did the Beckham Experiment Work?

Why was Beckham the right personality, and MLS the right league? Why was 2007 the right year? Why were the LA Galaxy the right team?

An outsider might say bringing Beckham to MLS was a no-brainer. The most visible player in the world comes to one of the world's greatest sport cities. Said athlete brings with him one of the world's top entertainers, who happens to be his spouse. The resulting math looks like this: *Football/Soccer + Los Angeles + Beckham + Victoria/Posh Spice + MLS + AEG = global success.*

Digging a little deeper, a similar equation had not proved accurate just a quarter century prior. *Football/Soccer + New York + Pelé + Warner Communications + NASL = national failure.*

The big difference was timing and the game's North American evolution. In the 1970s, soccer in North America was a sideshow with youth participation numbers low, fan interest lower, and immigration populations from soccer-loving countries modest. The 1994 World Cup had not happened yet. Women's soccer—where the United States has emerged as a dominant country and Canada as a serious contender—was just a dream.

But by 2007, things were much different. Soccer was the sport with the most youth participants, immigration had brought many soccer-loving fans to North America, and American women's soccer was the star team at World Cup and Olympic levels. The Canadian women were contenders.

Beckham, for his part, was the perfect catalyst for this tipping point. The 2002 movie, *Bend It Like Beckham*, helped introduce him to young North American audiences.

At thirty-one, he was still in his prime as a soccer player and celebrity. His athletic prowess and good looks made him popular in every corner of the globe. He'd spent about a decade with Manchester United, arguably the most storied franchise in all the sport, where he won numerous titles and accolades. He was a fixture and captain of England's national team. His ability to set up his teammates with extraordinary passes made for extraordinary sharable moments (just as YouTube took off in 2005).

During the six-year period from 2007 to 2012, Beckham wore the colors of the LA Galaxy and played in MLS. Over that time, he played 98 games producing one of his signature assists 40 times and scoring 18 goals. Even better, he helped the Galaxy capture two MLS Cups and that made a huge difference on the field and off.

For MLS, Beckham's decision to play in America was critically important to the league's long-range plan.

EXPERT PERSPECTIVE: SCOTT FRENCH, SOCCER JOURNALIST
How David Beckham Changed MLS

It's impossible to overstate David Beckham's importance to Major League Soccer and the league's immense growth—to America's soccer culture, too—following the iconic midfielder's arrival in 2007, no matter how myth (and marketing) informs the tale.

Without the English superstar's six seasons with the LA Galaxy, injuries or not, we don't have what we have today: a brimming supporters culture within an increasingly thriving MLS that has become a legitimate source of global-quality talent, with partnerships paving a lucrative future beyond the coming 2026 World Cup.

Beckham, possessing a unique blend of on-field gravitas and vast beyond-sport celebrity, brought legitimacy to a league in desperate need of it, greatly raising MLS's profile at home while drawing attention from around the world. He booted MLS into modernity and played a propulsive role in making the United States a genuine, or real, soccer nation.

No Beckham, no Messi.

Beckham made America's MLS cool. Along the way, he lured big money and new clubs to MLS, many of them with considerable aspirations and savvy front offices. He also opened a landscape that has, to rabid response, brought soccer's GOAT to MLS. (Oh, and Beckham did so literally, in 2023 signing the Argentine demigod for his own Inter Miami CF—one of the perks that came with his initial five-year, $32.5 million [not including incentives] contract, a mind-boggling sum in MLS's world at the time—and snagging a few more legends to play alongside him.)

No Beckham, maybe no MLS as of 2010.

The league's timeline is divided by his arrival. Before Beckham, a decade of intense economic struggle, hundreds of millions of dollars lost, and near-collapse. After Beckham, well, just take a look.

There are robust clubs in every corner of the country, from Beckham's Miami side—now the league's signpost team, as was the Galaxy during his time in LA—to the Seattle Sounders and Portland Timbers with their raucous support.

From Atlanta United and its huge crowds to Los Angeles FC, more successful since its start than its down-the-110-freeway rival. In Philly and Montreal and at Yankee Stadium. In unexpected places like Nashville, Cincinnati, Charlotte, and Austin.

Beckham showed up in a league with eleven teams, all of them shedding major cash. There are thirty clubs playing now and if profitability is still a ways off for many, all but four are valued at more than half a billion dollars. Four clubs, LAFC, Atlanta United, LA Galaxy, and Inter Miami are all valued at more than US$1 billion.

Had he never come, would MLS have survived the global financial meltdown waiting around the corner? Possibly not.

"We're either a dog in the middle of the lake doing the paddle to survive. Or we are going to shake this off, think big and change the league forever," said Tim Leiweke, who did most of the grunt work to get Beckham to Southern California. Talking to the *Los Angeles Times* in 2020 he added, "There was no one else on the face of the Earth that could have done what David Beckham did for Major League Soccer."

Beckham, MLS commissioner Don Garber once opined, was the "shot heard 'round the world."

It's true. He made the world take notice.

He made *players* around the world take notice, sparked their interest, and among those who followed in his wake—through the "Beckham rule," which enabled teams to sign "Designated Players" paid above, often well above, the permitted maximum salary—are some of the biggest names in the game: Zlatan Ibrahimović, Kaká, Thierry Henry, Steven Gerrard, Frank Lampard, Wayne Rooney, Gareth Bale, Giorgio Chiellini, Andrea Pirlo, Didier Drogba, David Silva, Rafa Marquez, Javier "Chicharito" Hernandez—and now Messi, his teammates Sergio Busquets, Luis Suarez, and Jordi Alba, plus new LAFC goalkeeper Hugo Lloris and striker Olivier Giroud. Imagine any of these latching on before Beckham.

"He was the one who set the standard and set the bar for people coming here," Irish striker Robbie Keane, who followed Beckham to the Galaxy, told *The Guardian* in 2013. "He certainly put MLS on the map. He's like the equivalent of Tiger Woods in golf. That's how I see it. That's the influence he's had on MLS, and a lot of people should be grateful for that."

A Complicated History
They certainly are in MLS's domain, but David Beckham's legacy is far more complicated, as is American soccer's. Beckham wasn't the first transformative force, or the greatest, in the sport's evolution on these shores. Nor was he the primary instigator of all he wrought.

Philip Anschutz, a billionaire businessman whose holdings since 1998 have included the LA Galaxy, is the central figure in Beckham's American adventure. Simon Fuller, Beckham's representative at 19 Entertainment, was the savvy marketer who amplified his presence. Bruce Arena, the greatest coach in American soccer annals, corralled the competing interests and created a champion.

Beckham followed in the footsteps of Pelé, the biggest name in the sport's history, and in the wash of the 1994 World Cup, the most incisive game-changer of all.

The sport has been played in America since before the Civil War, was part of a vivid culture since at least the 1880s, but existed for more than a century largely as an immigrant sport played in ethnic enclaves, most famously in the northeast and St. Louis. There have always been talented players, and the country has prospered from their skills—never more so than in the national team's semifinal run at the first World Cup, in 1930, and in the shattering upset of mighty England twenty years later—to nearly zero notice at home.

The path toward where we sit now began in 1967, when a dozen foreign clubs, most of them English or Scottish, were imported to play in the United Soccer Association. The new league was spawned by excitement surrounding England's 1966 World Cup title and backed by some big-four-sport bigwigs—the likes of Lamar Hunt, Henry Clay Ford, and Jack Kent Cooke—and these clubs were provided new monikers (Boston Rovers, New York Skyliners, Vancouver Royal Canadians, and such) and sent onto their respective pitches.

The Houston Stars (Brazil's Bangu AC) drew nearly 35,000 for one game, but the league average was fewer than 8,000. The title game, a raucous overtime clash in which the Los Angeles Wolves (Wolverhampton Wanderers) pulled out a 6–5 triumph over the Washington Whips (Aberdeen FC), was seen by 17,842 at LA's Memorial Coliseum. Not bad, considering.

The United States merged with another league known as the National Professional Soccer League (NPSL) a year later to form the NASL, with no discernible impact on mainstream America's indifference.

That changed in 1975, when the New York Cosmos signed Pelé, the one soccer star whose name a decent percentage of Americans knew. He was bigger than the sport over here, and his arrival is the real start—a huge piece of it, at least—of what exists now.

The Brazilian superstar was a sensation, filling stadiums, enticing newcomers to the game, and inspiring more legends to migrate. The NASL suddenly had cachet. (The 2006 documentary *Once in a Lifetime: The Extraordinary Story of the New York Cosmos* is recommended viewing.)

The league would falter a decade later, long after Pelé had departed, destroyed by overeager expansion and silly spending. A dozen years would pass before a proper replacement—Major League Soccer—was established, but America's relationship with the game had grown exponentially during the NASL's seventeen-year tenure. Much of the credit goes elsewhere.

The NASL's rise coincided with and was expanded by the start of the youth soccer boom, prodded primarily by the American Youth Soccer Organization (AYSO), founded in 1964 in Southern California, and its fierce expansion across the country through the 1970s. Soccer all of a sudden was something kids played.

It's how most of my generation got its start in the game. AYSO arrived in Orange County, southeast of LA, in 1971, when I was nine, and from that point, soccer was what I played. My neighborhood was filled with soccer players. Other places increasingly were, too.

This youth boom provided a missing foundation, creating a burgeoning community that understood and enjoyed and played or watched the sport. If not all of them became huge fans—the United States already had its major sports, of course—they gave the game a foothold, and the generations to follow would grow closer ties.

The decade following the NASL's demise and leading to MLS's creation might be the most important in the sport's history here. The rise of competitive youth club soccer, at a level far beyond AYSO's "everybody plays" ethic, began producing some real talent, and the United States, with a college-age mix of youth-boom products, the sons of immigrants, and those who arrived from elsewhere in childhood, came within one game of qualifying for the 1986 World Cup. Three years later, FIFA awarded the 1994 World Cup to the United States in hopes of opening a lucrative market to the game. That accelerated everything.

First the Americans, with a Paul Caligiuri miracle in Port-of-Spain, Trinidad, squeezed into the 1990 tournament in Italy, their first World Cup in forty years. They lost all three games but gave the hosts a real battle, and preparations for 1994 soon followed. Nobody can put on a show like the Yanks, it was said, and the world got what it wanted: a brilliantly organized event with more butts in seats than ever before, a rabid home audience providing its core. And the United States, hardly a powerhouse, made it to the knockout stage.

Soccer, finally, had arrived, no matter the nonsense a caustic, out-of-touch generation of old-school newspaper columnists concocted. Where it would go depended on many things, most of all the 1996 arrival of MLS, established as part of the agreement to bring the World Cup to America. There was great hope—there were true believers—but no certainties.

The league brought in some big names from the start, but, like the superstars who flocked to the NASL, so many were on their career downslopes. MLS was portrayed as a "retirement" league, and there was some truth to that.

There also was decent talent, from home and abroad, but little depth. A drop-off in level was visible after the first dozen to fourteen players on most rosters. From a global perspective, an American league was a good thing, and the rise of the U.S. national team with an expanding player presence on the European club landscape—and especially after Bruce Arena took charge following the dismal 1998 World Cup performance—was warmly welcomed, but the best leagues and players were, unquestionably, in Europe, and what happened here had few reverberations.

MLS owners were shedding multiple millions every year with no end in sight, and the league contracted by two teams after the 2001 season. The end appeared near.

Anschutz's Gamble

The most important figure in MLS's nearly three decades, the primary impetus for its progression into an increasingly sustainable major sports league, is Anschutz, one of the league's founders and its most vital and influential club owner. He believed in soccer as many hadn't, with his wallet.

When it looked like MLS wasn't going to make it, he stepped up, increasing his holdings from three teams—the Galaxy, Colorado Rapids, and Chicago Fire—to six of the league's ten. He began building soccer-specific stadiums, starting with the Galaxy's home on the Cal State Dominguez Hills campus in Carson, California, that could provide previously unavailable revenue streams, opening a window to a potentially prosperous future.

"Without Phil Anschutz," Garber said the year before Beckham arrived, "there's no MLS today."

Anschutz quelled the storm, and with the league finally on solid footing, at least for the short-term, he (and Garber, a former NFL official recruited to the league in 1999) were ready to pursue greater ambitions. Here's where Beckham steps into the tale.

MLS was barely a blip on the world stage. Nobody really paid attention, aside from MLS fans, and there were only so many of them. The league needed to be bigger and better, and that required the kind of talent—and a certain level of star power, on and off the field—that was in short supply.

Beckham had that talent. More so, he had celebrity.

There were better, more complete players on the planet, with Ronaldinho and Kaká and Thierry Henry around and Messi and Cristiano Ronaldo starting to take over. There was nobody in the game more famous, maybe Pelé and Diego Maradona aside.

And maybe not: Beckham was a superstar on the field, deservedly revered for that precise, brilliant right foot. He also was an iconic figure away from the game, a name—with a gorgeous face and figure to go with it—that resonated with many who couldn't care a whit about the sport.

He'd grown up in East London dreaming of playing for Manchester United, the club his father worshipped, and caught the club's attention at sixteen. He was a keen attacker with one otherworldly skill: the ability to place a ball from any distance on an exact spot with his right foot. Deadly on set pieces, decisive in open play, and with a marvelous foundation: a blue-collar work ethic, savvy attention to detail, and an immense soccer IQ. He made his first-team debut at seventeen, saw his first UEFA Champions League action two years later, then got into a Premier League game a month before his twentieth birthday.

Beckham was part of a golden generation of young players to make a huge impact as Manchester United, under (his father figure and soon-to-be-knighted) Alex Ferguson, established a dynasty that would capture thirteen league titles, two Champions League, and four F.A. Cup titles over twenty-one seasons. He established himself on the right side of midfield in the 1995–1996 campaign, helping the club to the Premier League/FA Cup double, then blew up when he scored a spectacular goal at Wimbledon on Opening Day of the following season, an arcing, bending shot from just beyond the midfield stripe that sailed over goalkeeper Neil Sullivan and into the net.

That made him a star. His good looks and East London charm drew added attention, and his romance with Victoria Adams—"Posh Spice" from the superstar Spice Girls pop group—made him tabloid fodder, their celebrity statures morphing into something far greater. They were, as his close friend and United teammate Gary Neville put it in Netflix's *Beckham* documentary miniseries (also recommended), "the new Charles and Diana, in some ways. They were like royalty."

Beckham prospered, mostly, on the field with Man United and England's national team, which he would captain on fifty-nine occasions. He was twice runner-up for FIFA's World Player of the Year honor, and a 2003 move to Real Madrid, arguably the world's biggest club, amplified his stature. Adams, whom he would marry in 1999, four months after the birth of their first child, had turned him into a fashion icon and opened to him a world beyond the field, where his celebrity outpaced that of movie stars and rock idols and royalty, his queen excepted. He was a god, almost literally: His statue sits just below the altar in a Bangkok Buddhist temple.

That the real Beckham, a decent, blue-collar guy, cut against this grain made him all the more attractive. He was no diva.

California-Bound

The list of players who could move the needle on all fronts—whose celebrity transcended the sport—began and ended with Beckham. Anschutz instructed Leiweke, then the president of Anschutz's sports and entertainment company, to reel him in, whatever the cost. It required intense work—both romancing the English super-star, who was set to leave Real Madrid, and creating a mechanism dubbed the "Beckham Rule," enabling MLS teams to sign "Des-ignated Players" that would otherwise surpass MLS's maximum salary (for an individual player) limits and push clubs past the tight salary cap—to make it possible.

That pursuit and its success changed MLS and soccer in America in bold ways, but it was largely about marketing, at the start. In fact, the whole Beckham project was about marketing: to mainstream America, the soccer world, even the planet at large. The splash mattered more than the substance, and what a splash it was, to Beckham's and MLS's prosperity.

It was sports as entertainment—a relatively recent but increas-ingly accepted philosophy—and a wedding of sport, of MLS, of *Beckham*, to Hollywood, and it began with a leak from Beckham's reps, before his Galaxy pact was announced in January 2007, that the deal was worth $250 million. (It wasn't. That was what they'd internally predicted he'd make from his revenue sources over the course of the contract.)

There would also be huge headlines, of course, and a hero's welcome when introduced at a star-studded event inside the Galaxy's stadium covered by seven hundred media from as far away as Germany and Japan.

"This is big," it all screamed, and the media bit hard.

The Beckhams were news. Everywhere.

They found a home in Beverly Hills, were immediately fêted by Hollywood's elite—old chum Tom Cruise, Will Smith, Stevie Wonder, and others at a lavish to-do—and the In-N-Out Burger forays made for fun fodder on TMZ. The stars turned out in droves for sold-out Galaxy games, watching from field seats or luxury boxes. There was no telling who insiders might run into in the hallways surrounding the locker rooms.

On the field and in the Galaxy's front office, things weren't so cozy. There were chemistry issues, an abysmal record before Arena took command late in the 2008 campaign, and injuries and commitments elsewhere—most notoriously off-and-into-season loans to AC Milan (and stated desire after the first to remain in Italy)—that limited Beckham to fewer than a dozen games in half of his six seasons. Much of that territory is amply covered in the late, great Grant Wahl's 2009 book, *The Beckham Experiment*, a tome Beckham despised.

He wasn't fully trusted by the club's fans until his last two years, when he was brilliant as LA romped to successive MLS Cup titles. That made up for all that had gone wrong before and cemented his legacy with the club, all celebrated (or culminated) with the 2019 unveiling of his statue outside the Galaxy stadium.

The Galaxy had been one of MLS's initial success stories, right from the start, when it drew more than 69,000 fans to the Rose Bowl for its 1996 debut, won its first twelve games, and played in the first MLS Cup, letting a late two-goal lead disappear in a rain-soaked, 3–2 overtime loss to D.C. United.

The Galaxy featured a team of stars, starting with colorful Mexican goalkeeper Jorge Campos and 1994 World Cup winger Cobi Jones, and made it to two more championship games before finally claiming its first league title in 2002.

Landon Donovan, the biggest of American soccer stars, arrived in 2005 and carried the club, after a problematic regular season, to another MLS Cup crown. Things quickly went sour, right around the time discussions with Beckham's reps commenced.

LA missed the playoffs for the first time in 2006 and were worse in 2007, with little seen of Beckham, who aggravated an existing injury in his debut, a July friendly against Chelsea, and made just five league appearances.

The low point came the following year under Ruud Gullit, a legendary Dutch player who had seen success as a manager in England but was ill-suited for MLS, with its arcane rules and his strategic shortcomings. He had been brought in by Beckham's people, who were effectively running the club at that point, to the dismay of general manager Alexi Lalas. (For greater detail, check out Wahl's book.)

There was discord within the team, and Gullit and Lalas were gone before summer was done, with Arena stepping into both jobs. Thus began the club's greatest era, one marked by three MLS Cup championships, four Western Conference titles, and two Supporters' Shields (for the league's best regular-season record) in eight seasons.

Arena himself was a legend by this point.

He'd won five NCAA titles in a six-year span at Virginia before taking charge at D.C. United, where he won the first two MLS Cups. He then stepped into the national team post, building a side that dominated archrival Mexico, for the first time, through most of the next decade, guided it to the quarterfinals (with a win en route over Mexico) at the 2002 World Cup, captured two CONCACAF Gold Cup titles, and drew with champion-to-be Italy during a disappointing but undervalued showing at the 2006 World Cup.

Arena is the biggest personality in any room he steps into, and there was never any question about who was in charge once he arrived. Getting his two biggest stars on the same page was of paramount importance, but Beckham and Donovan's relationship deteriorated following the publication of Wahl's book and some of the American star's comments within.

Arena told the two to work it out, pronto, and that was that. Donovan apologized for not keeping his thoughts in-house while backing their content, Beckham accepted, and their partnership developed into something special, more so once Keane, a natural goal scorer, joined in 2011.

Beckham's abilities truly began to serve the Galaxy on the field that season. He was fully committed, and the details of his game—how hard he worked in midfield, his combativeness, his intelligence and vision, and, of course, that cultured right foot—fed LA's success. The Galaxy went 19–5–10 to win the Shield, then mowed down three playoff foes, the Houston Dynamo in the final, for the club's third MLS championship.

Beckham departed after another title the next year, concluding his playing career with six months at French powerhouse Paris-Saint Germain.

Beckham's Legacy

Leiweke sold Beckham on the Galaxy and MLS with a simple idea: How often does the opportunity arrive to chart new ground, to build the foundation for something truly meaningful, to bridge the world's game to the world's most lucrative market at its most essential level? There's only one major-league sport across the planet; here's the chance to make it major-league, *truly* major-league in America.

Beckham couldn't say no, and so here we are, more than a few steps on the trot toward that reality. MLS grew up during Beckham's time in LA. He was the trigger, galvanizing those working alongside him, attracting new and deep-pocketed blood, lighting the flame that the rest of the world, blind to this point, would not ignore.

Before Beckham, the dark ages. With Beckham, the world's attention.

"The first time I heard about [MLS] was when Beckham signed with the Galaxy, and it went worldwide," said Swedish superstar Zlatan Ibrahimović, who would spend a couple of seasons with the Galaxy before the pandemic. "I mean, when David does something, the whole world knows about it. And him signing with MLS became global news. It became interesting and attractive."

"David showed the world that it's good to play here and opened up [our] eyes," continued Ibrahimović. "The US market is maybe the biggest in the world, and if you have this sport here and make it as big as basketball—or like [soccer is] in Europe—it will become a big thing."

The moment Beckham signed up, everybody knew the Galaxy, knew MLS. The world paid attention, more top players looked to make the move, and each step advanced the cause, with further waves of players arriving from Europe and South America.

And not just superstars: MLS has become a launching pad to Europe for young Latin American talent—for some European talent, too—and as a viable option for veterans taking the next step in their careers, with a lot of them sticking around and making their homes here, their presence greatly improving the level of play.

A rush to join the league, starting with the Seattle Sounders, a club tied to a long, rich history, and towering fan base. Then, a new team in Philadelphia, plus the Sounders' longtime Cascadia rivals in Portland and Vancouver, and a team in Montreal in Beckham's final season.

The real boom would follow his tenure, a dozen additions across the country, and especially in the Southeast, over a decade as franchise fees rocketed from $30–$40 million to the $500 million San Diego spent to join the party.

The list of current and past investors/operators includes the New York Yankees and Manchester City FC's parent company (New York City FC), NFL owners Arthur Blank (Atlanta United FC) and David Tepper (Charlotte FC), the late MLB owner Peter Seidler (San Diego FC), and Bill Hagerty (Nashville SC), who late became a Tennessee senator.

All in all, Beckham is largely responsible for:

- A vibrant supporters culture that has blossomed around nearly every club, some of them spectacularly so—Seattle and Portland, LAFC and Atlanta, Austin and Charlotte, Philadelphia and Kansas City, Cincinnati and Orlando, Nashville and Minnesota—with game-day atmospheres remindful of what is seen elsewhere, but without hooligans.

- The rise of developmental academies at every club, recruiting and honing essential talent for their first teams—the aim of clubs the world over—and creating valuable assets to be sold to top foreign clubs. Much of America's current golden generation that have impressed for clubs overseas while leading a national team that can compete more fully with the world's best has come from these academies.

- The maturation of the league's technical departments, with greater emphasis on global scouting—and scores of resulting success stories—and analysis, improved strength and conditioning practices, enhanced nutrition and health, and, vitally, greater tactical sophistication and game-model development. Foreign coaches who once struggled to succeed in MLS, with its arcane roster rules and lesser skill, are playing a major role in advancing the game here, along with a lengthening list of young American coaches bred on MLS fields.

- Closer relationships with clubs and leagues overseas, particularly with Mexico's Liga MX and the Leagues Cup competition with Mexican clubs that began in 2023. There's

Manchester City's involvement in NYCFC—both are owned by City Football Group, which has clubs in more than a dozen countries—and Red Bull GmbH's as owner of the New York Red Bulls, where Jesse Marsch got his start as manager in 2015 before shifting to RB Leipzig and Red Bull Salzburg from 2019 to 2021, the beverage company's top two teams. He later coached Leeds United and in May 2024 was named head coach of Canada's national team. And the American ownership boom in European clubs kicked off with Colorado Rapids owner Stan Kroenke's takeover of London powerhouse Arsenal FC shortly after Beckham's arrival.

- A series of lucrative partnerships and sponsorship deals with some of the largest companies on the planet—the biggest with adidas—leading to a landmark, ten-year, $2.5 billion "television" deal with streaming service Apple TV.

- Another Beckham. Well, sort of: Lionel Messi, the most revered player on the planet, maybe the greatest ever to take the field, has brought MLS another spotlight; one even brighter than Beckham's, given Apple TV's global availability, the league's greater profile on the American sporting landscape, and soccer's global commercial advances during the past dozen years. It has provided a well-illuminated path for the next phase of MLS's growth.

The Argentine maestro is the biggest thing MLS has seen and the only possible candidate to lead MLS on its next leap. That might be so, but much of it benefited from Beckham's commitment to MLS. Inter Miami is his club—that first contract gave Beckham the right to establish a club when his playing days were done—and Messi became his prize recruit. Beckham's legacy (on behalf of MLS) continues.

CHAPTER SEVEN

MLS in Miami

How Lionel Messi Made Inter Miami a Global Brand

THE TITLE OF THIS BOOK PAINTS MLS AS A GLOBAL GIANT. A LEGITI-mate contender among well-established front runners. An entity known regardless of language spoken, culture, or corner of the globe.

This chapter aims to support this reality and the importance of star players' roles in helping move a sport (or a league) with financial stability and toward global recognition.

THE EARLY HISTORY OF PRO SOCCER IN FORT LAUDERDALE

Our starting point is Fort Lauderdale, Florida. Known for its geographical position on the Atlantic coast, spectacular beaches, boating canals, and great weather, this city of nearly two hundred thousand people is equal parts sought-after retirement location and escape destination because of its entertainment and outdoor activities. Some have called it the Venice of North America, with its more than one hundred miles of "boating roads" or canals to navigate the city.

Fort Lauderdale provides a little taste of southern Italy on the southeast coast of the United States.

The city is home to Lockhart Stadium, built in the late 1950s for high school sports and renovated many times since. On and off since 1977, this stadium has been home to multiple professional soccer clubs.

So, let's go back in time.

Imagine, for a moment, it's 2018, and consider an average sports fan who is living in Fort Lauderdale. Statistically, they reside in the larger Miami metro area, with downtown Miami about thirty miles away. Miami has a population base of more than six million and, according to U.S. Census data, is the eighth largest metro area in the United States.

Sport matters in Miami at both the professional and NCAA level. The NFL's Miami Dolphins, the NBA's Miami Heat, and MLB's Miami Marlins are legendary American football, basketball, and baseball franchises with championships, established brands, and deep fanbases.

The NHL's Florida Panthers, a hockey team with periods of modest success, play just west of Fort Lauderdale. In 2024, the Panthers had one of their best seasons ever reaching the Stanley Cup Final and winning the Cup in a close seven-game series over the Edmonton Oilers. At the college level, three universities (Miami, Florida Atlantic, and Florida International) all offer D1 sports at the highest levels.

If you were a soccer fan in 2018 in Fort Lauderdale—which was not all that common at the time—you would have been aware of the Fort Lauderdale Strikers, who ceased operations just two years prior, in 2016, after an on-and-off existence since 1977 (including some years with star-studded rosters alongside relocations and ongoing financial issues).

A highlight was the 1979 to 1981 period where the late Gerd Müller, still the all-time leading goal scorer in the German Bundesliga, starred for the team and led them to the 1980 North American Soccer League (NASL) championship game, where the Strikers lost to the New York Cosmos, the most famous of all NASL franchises. The Cosmos won five championships in fifteen years and was Pelé's final club from 1975 to 1977.

Müller was one of the greatest players of his generation, if not ever.

In addition to his still leading the Bundesliga all-time scoring list by more than fifty goals, he also starred for his country, West Germany, winning a World Cup, the European Championship, and setting various goal scoring records along the way. He scored more than a goal a game for his country and still ranks among the top three international goal scorers when looking at a goals-per-game ratio.

A list (below) of his further achievements is nothing but impressive:

- 1970 Ballon d'Or (world's top player).
- 1970 European Footballer of the Year.
- Top scorer and Golden Boot winner at the 1970 FIFA World Cup (10 goals) where West Germany finished third.
- 1972 European Championships top goal scorer, leading West Germany to the title.
- 1974 FIFA World Cup winning goal, giving West Germany the title.

Until Brazilian star Ronaldo scored his fifteenth FIFA World Cup goal in 2006, Müller was the leading FIFA World Cup goal scorer at fourteen, a spot he held for thirty-two years. On numerous occasions, he has been named to the top players of all-time lists.

But back to the story of soccer in Fort Lauderdale and the Strikers.

For each of the 1977 to 1983 seasons, including the three Müller years, the Strikers performed well on the field, qualified for the postseason, and featured many star players beyond Müller. However, and this was characteristic of soccer in many U.S. cities until very recently, the club was forced in 1984 to relocate to Minneapolis, Minnesota's largest city, keeping their club name, and becoming the Minnesota Strikers.

They played the 1984 NASL season, then moved to the Major Indoor Soccer League for the 1984 to 1988 period, ceasing operations due to financial difficulties following the 1988 season.

Back in South Florida in 1984, the upstart United Soccer League (USL) launched, and a new club was started in Fort Lauderdale by Ronnie Sharp, a former Strikers player, who signed a number of his former teammates to play for the club. The on-field success of the Fort Lauderdale Sun was strong but short-lived. The team and the league only lasted two seasons, with the second season cut short.

In 1988, the same ownership group of the original Fort Lauderdale Strikers launched a new franchise, with the same name, as part of the new (but third version of a league with the name) American Soccer League.

As part of a merger with the Western Soccer League, the club joined the American Professional Soccer League in 1990, merged with the Orlando Lions in 1991 (keeping the Strikers name and brand), then folded (again) in 1994, the same year the United States hosted the FIFA World Cup for the first time.

The Strikers' on-field success was high during this period, winning two championships in 1989, both the American Soccer League and the National Pro Soccer championship.

Despite the challenges the Strikers and their leagues had faced in the early 1990s, another team began playing in 1994 as part of the United States Interregional Soccer League. Dubbed the Fort Lauderdale Kicks, they played alongside the Strikers in 1994, meaning Fort Lauderdale actually had two soccer teams, two major tenants, that year.

Interestingly, following the failure of the American Professional Soccer League in 1994, the Kicks were rebranded as the Strikers. They then changed again to the Florida Strikers for the 1996 season before folding the following year. The trend of failed clubs and leagues up to this point is clear.

The 1998 Debut of MLS in Miami

Contrary to what most "new" soccer fans think, MLS existed in the Miami area before and in Fort Lauderdale specifically. In the league's first round of expansion in 1997, the Miami Fusion became one of two new clubs awarded a franchise. A year later they joined the league.

The Fusion played in Fort Lauderdale for four seasons—1998 to 2001—and had MLS's best regular season record in 2001, an accomplishment recognized by the awarding of the Supporters' Shield, an annual award given out by the league.

The MLS Supporters' Shield is an interesting story in and of itself.

At launch, MLS aligned with most North American professional sport leagues by establishing a regular season followed by playoffs to award the league championship. This, however, differed from the traditional soccer format, which awards the league championship to the top point-getter in the regular season. The five major European leagues use this format, as do all the leagues in Mexico, Central America, and South America. Thus, based on the interest of many fans, the Shield was first awarded in 1999, the fourth MLS season by the Independent Supporters' Council with the support of the MLS, with the 1996 to 1998 regular season champions receiving the award retroactively. The Independent Supporters' Council is self-funded by supporters of MLS clubs and they have awarded the Shield every year since.

While the Fusion excelled on the field, the club struggled with ticket sales and financials. Thus, following its fourth and final season, MLS shut the club down.

During its four-year run, the Fusion led a renovation of Lockhart Field, the longtime home of the Strikers, and built it into a 20,000 soccer-specific stadium.

Once again, soccer in Miami had failed, and this time at the MLS level.

Despite a tremendous start to the Fusion, with more than 20,000 fans at their sold-out inaugural game of 1998, and an additional 3,000 fans turned away from Lockhart Stadium that day, the team failed. Interest from fans declined rapidly, even with a decent on-the-field product highlighted by star players, and a playoff berth. Average attendance hovered around 10,000 per game at the end of the season.

The following two seasons, 1999 and 2000, were characterized by poor results both on and off the field. Thus, even with the Shield and a semi-final appearance in 2001, the club's financial situation and subpar attendance (fourth worst in the league in 2001) led to the league's decision to contract the club and cease operations.

Commissioners of major sports leagues would probably agree that franchise contraction is dangerous both internally and externally. There are many factors, but—in a nutshell—it is indicative of both a market where the club failed and the reality that no other owner or new buyer is willing to purchase the club. Additionally, other current owners may question the league's solvency.

There are additional factors.

First, public reports at the time suggested the Fusion had the lowest season ticket sales and sponsorship revenues in MLS.

Second, the league was still in its early stages and fragile. A 2005 *New York Times* article by John Eligon indicated the league had lost more than a quarter billion dollars in its first five years of existence.

Finally, reports—including one from Jeff Bradley in his *ESPN The Magazine* 2000 article—noted that the Fusion ownership group was operating on a low-spend model, not aligned with other MLS owners and the league, who wanted investments to fuel growth.

Thus, in early 2002, the league announced the Fusion, along with the MLS team in Tampa Bay, would both terminate operations, bringing MLS back to ten clubs for the 2002 season. This led to a flurry of conversations, media coverage, and soccer analysts discussing the failure of soccer in Florida. Although none of the reasons on the list below are drawn from fully reliable sources, the emerging themes include elements of the following:

- Lack of an ownership group willing to invest.
- Lack of a soccer-specific stadium in downtown Miami.
- Hot summer weather (not ideal for fans inside the venue).
- Florida's rainy season coincides with the MLS season.
- Florida's population is greatest in winter when MLS is not playing.
- A transient Florida population.
- Much like the Bay Area of California, difficulty in associating the club with the many geographies of southeast Florida.
- The prominence of American football in the state.
- The rise of the NBA's Miami Heat at the time.
- The growth of professional ice hockey in Florida.

The Miami Fusion brand would surface one more time—in the form of a fourth-tier club playing in the National Premier Soccer League from 2015 until it folded in 2018.

The 2024 MLS season saw clubs draw an average of more than twenty-three thousand fans per game.

Games regularly draw very large crowds, sometimes more than seventy thousand.

Supporters' clubs around the league consist of deeply loyal fans who showcase their fandom loyalty.

COURTESY OF MAJOR LEAGUE SOCCER

MLS players make up one of the most diverse athlete populations in sport.
COURTESY OF MAJOR LEAGUE SOCCER

Top talent from all corners of the globe are attracted to MLS.
COURTESY OF MAJOR LEAGUE SOCCER

The continued role of David Beckham (shown here with Commissioner Don Garber) in MLS, from player to owner, has been instrumental to the league's success.
COURTESY OF MAJOR LEAGUE SOCCER

Lionel Messi's arrival has attracted global stars such as Will Smith (shown here with David Beckham at an Inter Miami game).
COURTESY OF MAJOR LEAGUE SOCCER

Commissioner Don Garber and Apple's senior vice president of Services, Eddy Cue, discuss the MLS Season Pass on Apple TV.
COURTESY OF MAJOR LEAGUE SOCCER

Apple TV's Season Pass coverage includes the *MLS 360* whip-around show.
COURTESY OF MAJOR LEAGUE SOCCER

Toronto FC—The focus of chapter 11 of this book—won the MLS Cup in 2017.
COURTESY OF MAJOR LEAGUE SOCCER

The LA Galaxy—led by Landon Donovan (top photo) and David Beckham (below with Commissioner Garber)—is perhaps the club best known for its role in MLS's growth. The Galaxy won their sixth MLS Cup in 2024.

Lionel Messi takes a corner kick against the New England Revolution in front of a crowd of more than 65,000 fans at Gillette Stadium in Foxborough, Massachusetts.
COURTESY OF NEW ENGLAND REVOLUTION

Miami Fusion's Failure

The Miami Fusion played its first game in March 1998 and its last during October 2001, a span of four mostly unsuccessful seasons that make it the shortest-lived franchise in MLS history, just ahead of Tampa Bay (1996–2001) and Chivas USA (2005–2014).

By any measure, the Fusion failed in virtually every respect but two. The 2001 team coached by Ray Hudson played a brand of cultured soccer that to this day stands among the best the league has seen.

Secondly, and more importantly than how beautifully that team played, was the stadium the Miami Fusion called home— Lockhart Stadium in Fort Lauderdale.

Don't let "Miami" in the name fool you. The Fusion played one game in Miami, in 2001, a 4–3 win over Columbus before fourteen thousand fans in the Orange Bowl. That win climaxed a four-game stretch in which they scored eighteen goals.

Cell phone entrepreneur Ken Horowitz had paid $20 million to buy the Miami Fusion in April 1997 and the historic, seventy-five thousand-seat Orange Bowl was the intended home. The Orange Bowl offered a view of the downtown Miami skyline and was in line with the MLS start-up plan under its first commissioner, Doug Logan, to revitalize iconic American football stadiums such as the Cotton Bowl in Dallas and Rose Bowl in Pasadena. It would also place an MLS club at the geographic heart of Miami's large Hispanic population, except that most of that demographic at the time came from Cuba, where the preferred pastime is baseball.

As is customary though in South Florida soccer annals, teams that identify as Miami always end up playing in Fort Lauderdale. Always. It started with the Miami Toros becoming the Fort Lauderdale Strikers in the NASL under the ownership of Joe and Elizabeth Robbie, who founded the NFL's Miami Dolphins. It was repeated with the Fusion and given a third go-around in 2020 with

Inter Miami opening a "temporary" stadium and training facility at the original Lockhart site.

The Fusion's and MLS's best-laid plans of playing near Calle Ocho blew up quickly when Horowitz couldn't agree on a lease with the city of Miami officials. With the 1998 start-up roughly nine months away and negotiations imploding, Horowitz turned to Broward County soccer leader Eddie Rodger to map out a plan to play instead at Lockhart Stadium.

Inter Miami did the same with Rodger in 2019 when its owners, Jorge Mas and David Beckham, couldn't find a place to play in Miami-Dade. Lockhart was the home for the Strikers from 1977–1983, with a capacity of about 19,500 in its NASL heyday. The Strikers were one of the NASL's most successful and beloved franchises and Rodger was the team trainer, tending to the sprains and muscle pulls for such legends as Teofilo Cubillas, Gerd Muller, George Best, and Ray Hudson, who was the ultimate Lockhart legend.

By the time Rodger showed Lockhart's potential to Horowitz, it had been restored to its original eight-thousand-seat capacity as a high-school football stadium, with concrete stands on two sides. Working with Don Lockerbie, who later oversaw Inter Miami's reimagining of the Lockhart site, Horowitz created a $5 million blueprint to replicate the Strikers stadium capacity by adding bleacher seating in the end zones.

By September 1997, before ever playing a game in Miami, Horowitz had an agreement with Fort Lauderdale officials for a 20,450-seat soccer-specific stadium that was a forty-minute drive from downtown Miami. It would be the smallest stadium in MLS but quickly transformed the future road map for the league.

The Fusion opened its doomed epoch on March 15, 1998, before a sell-out crowd and a national television audience on ABC. About three thousand fans were turned away according to newspaper accounts. Despite every effort by Colombian midfield magician

Carlos Valderrama to spoon-feed clear goalscoring chances to his teammates, the Fusion lost 2–0 to league champion D.C. United. But that's not what should be remembered from that day. Rather, it was the reactions from those who watched or "lived" that first game at Lockhart Stadium (as reported in the next day's papers).

- MLS Commissioner Doug Logan: "This stadium is the prototype for the future of MLS."
- D.C. United coach Bruce Arena: "Today was tremendous, and the atmosphere is a model for MLS."
- Fusion defender Cle Kooiman: "This is the best stadium in the US. A very cozy atmosphere. You can't ask for anything more."
- Fusion defender Wade Webber: "As a child of the NASL, I've been waiting for a day like this for years. It was a dream of mine to play in a standing-room only stadium in the US. Today, we fulfilled that dream."
- D.C. defender Jeff Agoos: "The stadium here is intimate [and] the fans really feed off that. I hope Miami can keep it up."

The problem? "Miami" couldn't keep it up in Fort Lauderdale.

The Fusion's opening loss to D.C. United was a missed opportunity to get a packed stadium to rise in celebration for even a single goal, much less a win. The first three seasons featured more of the same as the crowds dwindled to under ten thousand per game. Not even the 2001 team, with MLS icons Preki, Nick Rimando, and Pablo Mastroeni playing Barcelona-style soccer under the charismatic Hudson, could save the Fusion, despite a spike in attendance.

Horowitz had paid four times more than the $5 million entry fee for the ten MLS teams that debuted in 1996. It was a high cost that put the Fusion in a financial hole it didn't overcome. However, by the time Horowitz pulled his money and his team out of Lockhart, he had shown his fellow owners at the time—Lamar Hunt, Phil Anschutz, Robert Kraft, John Kluge—that playing in small, crowded stadiums was far better than losing money in big, empty ones.

In 1999, Lamar Hunt contracted with Lockerbie to build Crew Stadium in Columbus with 22,555 seats. That was roughly one quarter of the 80,000-seat capacity of the team's first home, the Ohio State football stadium. The MLS stadium revolution was on.

By 2008, Real Salt Lake became the eighth MLS team to play in their own soccer-specific stadium, the $110 million Rio Tinto, which became America First Field in 2022. The 2024 season opened with twenty-two of twenty-nine MLS franchises playing in their own stadiums, including two in Los Angeles.

Nothing remains of the original Lockhart Stadium, and there isn't even a historic marker at the sixty-four-acre Inter Miami site built by Mas and Beckham. And yet, if not for Robbie's Strikers and Horowitz's Fusion paving the way in Fort Lauderdale, Inter Miami's start-up may have been pushed to 2025 when its permanent home in Miami is scheduled to open.

Put another way, without Lockhart providing a viable site for Mas-Beckham to launch Inter Miami in 2020, one must ask if Lionel Messi would have come to MLS in 2023?

We don't have to speculate because Lockhart's unique place in American soccer history made that possible.

Was the Fusion a failure? Absolutely. By the unforgivable standards of playing or going out of business, Horowitz came up short. But he didn't fail entirely and that made a massive difference for the MLS of the future.

Post-MLS Failure: The Return of the Strikers

Following the demise of the Fusion in early 2002, professional soccer was absent from the area until 2006, when a United Soccer Leagues club, called Miami FC, started playing out of Olympic Heights, moving to Fort Lauderdale in 2009, changing its name to the Fort Lauderdale Strikers in 2011 (the same year the club joined the next iteration of NASL). The Strikers reached the championships series in 2011, finishing as runner-up. The next two seasons were mediocre, followed by a very successful 2014, which included Brazilian soccer legend Ronaldo joining the ownership group and a return to the league championship and another runner-up result. In the hype of Ronaldo's being named as owner, a rumor—that never materialized—surfaced that he might play (he was in his late thirties) if he could get in shape.

This excitement was (again) short-lived, however, as reports of financial challenges began to emerge in 2016, followed by a complaint regarding unpaid loans, legal proceedings, and—eventually—the termination of the team before the 2017 season began. The legal issues went public with a loan complaint issued by another MLS owner, who won the case and the rights to the Fort Lauderdale Strikers brand.

However, despite all the considerable South Florida history, whispers and rumors were starting about a new club coming to Miami—one destined to become a global force.

Expert Perspective: Gabriel Gabor, MLS consultant

It's hard to comprehend how an MLS expansion club that existed for only four seasons (1998–2001) could generate such nostalgia within a community—so much so, that twenty-five years after its founding, a podcast called "25 for 25: The story of the Miami Fusion from those who lived it," enjoyed commercial and critical success.

The 2001 Supporter's Shield–winning team—coached by the flamboyant Ray Hudson and featuring legends including Preki, Alex Pineda Chacon, Diego Serna, Nick Rimando, Kyle

Beckerman, Pablo Mastroeni, Jim Rooney, Chris Henderson, Tyrone Marshall, Brian Dunseth, Ian Bishop, Carlos Llamosa, and others—was arguably the most competitive squad in MLS history, only to become one of two teams contracted by the league at the end of the 2001 season.

My first day as the Fusion's director of communications was January 5, 1998, just seventy days before the opening match against defending MLS champions D.C. United in a nationally televised afternoon match on ABC TV.

I get insanely jealous of current expansion teams because some have as long as two years to prepare for their launch, with fully established staffs already in place. We had just ten weeks to build a team, sell season tickets, expand, and remodel an old high school stadium, hire support staff, and create all the other elements that come with the launch of a franchise.

There simply weren't enough hours in the day to get the work done, and the pressure was real. We all worked six or even seven days a week, and in one instance, facing a deadline for our team media guide, I had to pull an all-nighter at the office.

The fact is, I couldn't sleep soundly for weeks leading up to the opener, as my mind raced all night thinking of all the work that had to get done in time for the opener.

From inception, we had our work cut out for us.

Weeks before I got there, negotiations broke down between our majority owner Ken Horowitz and the city of Miami to play our home games at the historic 75,000-seat Orange Bowl stadium near downtown. Left with little choice, the ownership elected to play its home games thirty-six miles north at Lockhart Stadium, former home of the NASL's Fort Lauderdale Strikers of the 1970s and 1980s, which was being used as a 10,000-seat high school football facility.

Credit to Ken, he poured millions of dollars into renovating the venue into a fan-friendly 20,000-seat soccer specific stadium.

Those of us at the front office were left with the challenging task of explaining to fans, media, and sponsors why "Miami" Fusion FC was playing in another county—far from South Florida's Hispanic base. The location became a big source of debate, with public opinion evenly split between those who believed Fort Lauderdale was the epicenter of South Florida soccer, and others who only saw a soccer future for Miami.

Opening day, March 15, 1998, was one of the proudest moments of my twenty-five-year career in sports. We sold out the venue! The excitement kept building all week as national and even global media made their way to South Florida for the match.

I remember BBC covering the training sessions at the stadium the day before the game and thinking that this was "big time." Concurrently, renovations continued at Lockhart until the last moment.

On gameday when my counterparts from the league and I showed up at the press box at 8 a.m. to begin setting up, there were construction workers sleeping on the floor who apparently worked all night on the final touches.

Talk about cutting it close. Though we lost 2–0, most of us at the club came away thinking we had created something very special.

Unfortunately, we quickly learned that selling the team's second home game was much more difficult than selling an opener. Despite having a global superstar like Colombia's Carlos "El Pibe" Valderrama and a competitive young team that made the playoffs, we struggled at the gate, which only further fueled the debate on the stadium's location.

By the end of that first year, we had become a family—the front office staff, players, technical staff, and even fans. To this day, many of us stay in touch.

The second and third seasons were highlighted by the 1999 departure of Valderrama, and the 2000 midseason appointment of Ray Hudson as head coach. Ray was a bona fide South Florida soccer legend who captained the original Fort Lauderdale Strikers, and up to that point, was the popular TV commentator for our local broadcasts.

He was brilliant on TV, an eloquent wordsmith who would describe the game as no other. The players immediately responded to Ray's vision and contagious enthusiasm, and despite missing the playoffs, we made it to the finals of the 2000 Lamar Hunt U.S. Open Cup where we eventually lost to our 1998 expansion brethren, the Chicago Fire, at Soldier Field.

Personally, I was also thrilled that season with the arrival of our new president and general manager, the late Doug Hamilton, who soon promoted me to VP of communications. Doug was a gifted person and a great professional, a friend and mentor I still miss.

By the time the 2001 season kicked off, I had already left the Fusion for the NBA, I enjoyed the season as a fan, catching games from the stands or on TV whenever possible. It finally looked like the club was clicking on all cylinders, with growing crowds and an entertaining team that was capturing the hearts and minds of the local sports scene on its way to posting the best regular season record.

The team was one game away from MLS Cup, when an overtime header by San Jose Earthquakes' Troy Dayak ended Miami's season in what unknowingly was the last play in the existence of the club.

What made it so painful for the Fusion faithful was that we finally had a contender, and the fans were responding. The team averaged 11,177 fans, which exceeded that of three other MLS teams.

Sadly, for Ken Horowitz and his investors, the club revenue was not what they expected, and with the prospect of losing millions more, and no buyers in sight, the league contracted Miami along with the Tampa Bay Mutiny.

If I could go back to the Fusion days, I'm not sure I would change much knowing we all did the best we could with the resources and market conditions of the time.

Still, the team's legacy lives in the long-term success of so many who were part of the organization. The list of players who have gone on to leadership positions in the league is impressive, led by goalkeeper Garth Lagerwey who is now the president of Atlanta United, midfielder Chris Henderson, who is Inter Miami's chief soccer officer and sporting director. Many more—too many to name—have coached at the highest level, including midfielder Pablo Mastroeni, the current head coach at Real Salt Lake.

The Fusion's legacy also carries on in the success of Inter Miami. It puts a smile on my face to see the pink Herons flourish at a new stadium on the same site where the Fusion once played, carrying on this community's great soccer tradition.

In my view, South Florida is, was, and will always be a great soccer town. There has been professional soccer in this market near continuously since the Miami Toros were established in 1972.

The NASL Fort Lauderdale Strikers were a commercial success until the league folded, and subsequent incarnations of the brand—in both outdoor and indoor leagues—continued to serve the local soccer fans until the Fusion's arrival.

While South Florida waited twenty years for MLS's return, the gap was filled by additional incarnations of the Strikers in the north, and Miami FC in the south. The future looks even more promising with Inter Miami's 2023 signing of the GOAT, Argentine Lionel Messi, and a brand-new state of the art soccer-specific stadium scheduled to open in late 2025 next to Miami International Airport.

For me, that time in Miami was the ride of a lifetime.

Inter Miami CF and Lionel Messi

If we return to our typical sports fan (from earlier in the chapter) in Fort Lauderdale in 2018, they are already aware soccer has failed frequently in Fort Lauderdale. They can probably recall the Fort Lauderdale Strikers and might remember the failed MLS club. They might know a few facts about Gerd Müller, Ray Hudson, and Ronaldo, but they probably haven't attended a game or watched one in its entirety on television.

If they'd ever thought about going to a game, they knew tickets were easy to come by and averaged around thirty dollars. On the secondary market, prices were almost equal to the original purchase price which meant no one needed advance planning to attend a game.

Fast forward to February 21, 2024. Inter Miami CF, now in its fifth season and second with global superstar Lionel Messi, launch the twenty-ninth regular season of MLS at sold-out Chase Stadium, the name of the newly built but temporary soccer-specific venue on the same location as Lockhart. It will be home to the club until its new venue, the soccer-specific Miami Freedom Park, opens in 2026. The 2024 season was a success for Messi and Inter Miami CF as they won the Supporters' Shield, he scored twenty goals and was credited with sixteen assists in fifteen games, and he was named league MVP.

The average ticket price is now more than three hundred dollars, a tenfold increase. The atmosphere is wild, fans are singing and cheering, lines to buy merchandise are impossibly long. The Messi effect is clear, and the list of growth indicators is impressive.

The price to see Messi at an away game in 2023 averaged $275 per ticket, grew to more than $600 in 2024, and is expected to smash records again in 2025. The club's list of sponsors extends beyond Chase to global brands like Royal Caribbean and adidas. Apple reports subscribers to MLS Season Pass on Apple TV are growing and contributing to a global subscriber base. *SportsPro* magazine reports more than 1 million streamers per game.

The average ticket price for any MLS game has more than doubled since Messi joined the league. According to *Sportico*, Inter Miami CF is worth more than $1 billion, and revenues have risen from $55 million in 2022 to $127 million in 2023. They easily exceeded that total in 2024 and are expected to soar even higher in 2025.

How was this growth possible after the failed attempts from 1970 to 2017? Why is soccer suddenly more interesting to the average MLS fan, when the league trailed well behind American football, baseball, basketball, and even ice hockey?

Part of the answer starts with David Beckham and his agent, Simon Fuller. Beckham gives full credit to Fuller for including a contractual clause to purchase an MLS club for $25 million in his five-year MLS contract to play with the LA Galaxy signed in 2007.

Although not formally announced until 2018, the potential for Inter Miami CF began with the contract signing that gave Beckham an option for club ownership in the future. Only in late 2013, after Beckham's retirement, was an announcement of an ownership group made by MLS, including Beckham, Fuller, the Mas brothers, Jorge and Jose Mas, Miami-based business leaders, and others who later dropped out. Beckham activated his option in February 2014, and discussions with municipal officials for a new stadium in Miami were initiated.

In 2018, it was formally announced Inter Miami FC would become the twenty-fifth MLS club and launch during the 2020 MLS season.

Fuller was bought out by Beckham in 2019, meaning an ownership syndicate of three (Mas, Beckham, and Mas) remained (and which is still in place as of 2025).

The inaugural 2020 season for the new club was delayed and shortened by the COVID-19 pandemic. The club's performance in its first four seasons was subpar at best, with losing records in all but the 2022 season, when the club went 14–14–6. The highlight of this time was Argentine striker Gonzalo Higuaín, who scored twenty-nine goals for the club in just over two seasons.

Things changed dramatically on June 5, 2023, with the club sitting in the bottom spot in its division, when Messi, arguably soccer's greatest soccer player, fresh from leading Argentina to the 2022 FIFA World Cup win months earlier, announced he would join Inter Miami FC.

Previous reports had suggested he was returning to Barcelona, where he had played most of his legendary career, or heading to Saudi Arabia for an extraordinary salary, as fellow star Cristiano Ronaldo had done.

It became official July 15, when Messi signed a two-and-a-half-year contract with Miami, forever changing the club and MLS. A press conference was held the next day and from there, things went off.

Secondary market ticket prices skyrocketed with some reports noting price tags at ten times face value on StubHub and Vivid Seats. Fanatics announced Inter Miami CF was its highest-selling merchandise.

In fact, Fanatics put out on its social media channels that the first twenty-four hours of sales of Messi's jersey beat the results for Lebron James, Tom Brady, and Cristiano Ronaldo's following their respective previous moves to new clubs. It was Fanatics' highest selling twenty-hour period ever. Inter Miami's social media following swelled to be among the top clubs in any sport anywhere.

In his first game with the club, on July 21, 2023, Messi came on as a late replacement, eventually scoring the game-winning goal on a spectacular free kick. The club, despite a poor record before Messi joined, including having lost their previous eleven games in a row, went on a winning streak and the club won its first ever title, the Leagues Cup, in August.

In winning that championship, Inter Miami went undefeated in seven games, with five wins and two draws, as compared to their MLS regular season mark (most before Messi arrived) of 9–18–7.

In total, Messi played in 14 games for Inter Miami in 2023, starting 11, and netted 11 goals. Later that fall, Messi won his record eighth Ballon d'Or as the best soccer player in the world, the first time an active MLS player ever received that honor.

The 2024 season was also a successful campaign for Messi in Miami. Although he missed some time due to injury, he was the league's MVP, winning the Landon Donovan MLS MVP trophy. Miami captured the Supporters' Shield as the top regular season club but exited the playoffs in a first-round loss.

The evidence is clear. Since starting for Inter Miami in 2023, Messi has accelerated the league's rise and made it a global brand.

As an example, in the second game of his second season (February 25, 2024), hosted by the LA Galaxy, one of the league's best-known franchises in arguably the top soccer market in the United States, a number of new MLS records were set, which we share here:

First was the attendance record for the twenty-one-year-old venue, now known as Dignity Health Sports Park (27,642).

Second, as noted in *Sport Business Journal*, the game became the "highest-grossing game in stadium history." The club maxed out its media passes. Hollywood stars filled the stands, including actors, rappers, tennis players, basketball stars, politicians, and more A-listers than an MLS game had ever attracted.

As if scripted, Messi scored an extra-time goal to tie the game 1–1 for Miami, and it was impossible to tell who the home team was from the crowd's reaction.

At the club level, expectations, stated publicly, were that the club expected revenues would exceed $200 million in 2024, and Inter Miami's billion-dollar valuation would continue climbing during 2025, making Miami among the twenty-five most valuable global soccer clubs.

That's not all.

Backorders for Messi jerseys frequently existed with long wait times, and new sign-ups for Apple's MLS Season Pass were consistently linked to Messi.

CHAPTER EIGHT

MLS Expansion

The When, Where, and Why of MLS Growth

IS THERE AN OPTIMAL NUMBER OF TEAMS FOR MLS?

As the 2025 MLS season began, MLS reached a balanced state (i.e., an even number of teams) when its thirtieth team, San Diego FC, began play in Snapdragon Stadium. Almost immediately, though, wild rumors began circulating that MLS wanted (and was headed toward) two divisions of sixteen, bringing the league total to thirty-two clubs.

Many readers might ask why MLS would seek further expansion. One of the reasons given (generally from outsiders) is because the NFL and NHL have thirty-two. If the NFL has thirty-two, then surely, that's the optimal number.

While that simplistic logic is flawed, cities such as Sacramento, St. Louis, Las Vegas, Charlotte, Calgary, Indianapolis, Ottawa, Louisville, and Phoenix have previously thrown their hands in the air as cities interested in securing an MLS franchise or because the growth of their regional soccer fan base would seemingly guarantee success for a new club's ticket and sponsorship sales.

"Expansion is one of MLS's key goals, since adding more teams will help widen the fan base," wrote Catherine Ake of the Harris Poll in 2024. "Eventually, they hope to become one of the best professional soccer leagues in the world."

Ake noted that while MLS featured only ten teams in 1996 and now features thirty, "it is easier to grow a passionate MLS fanbase in cities and states with a professional soccer team." This happens in large part because "'Trial' interest grows in states with newer teams."

There is, of course, a risk to overexpanding or expanding too quickly because failure of a team (i.e., bankruptcy, inability to build a new stadium, a misreading of the fan base) requires the league to purchase the failing enterprise or to contract. This has happened with MLB having to buy the Montreal Expos (ultimately moving them to Washington, DC, in 2005) or the NHL owning and operating the Phoenix Coyotes from 2009 to 2013. Even worse than the league needing to purchase one of its own teams is contraction, where the league is reduced in size. This happened to MLS in 2001 when Fort Lauderdale and Tampa were contracted with MLS, reducing its size from twelve to ten teams. Both situations have negative consequences for the asset valuations of existing teams and future expansion.

To be sure, thirty-two is not a magic number and multiple North American professional sports leagues (as of 2025) have existed with fewer teams. Expansion is, however, a valuable way for a league to grow its appeal (by creating new excitement), and to benefit its owners (via a one-time expansion fee payment). Typically, a new club will pad the wallets of existing team owners. No less an authority than Commissioner Garber indicated in 2019 he believed MLS would eventually reach thirty-two (Nicholson, 2019). The table below outlines the current status of the major North American leagues with respect to expansion.

League	Teams	Most Recent Expansion
NFL	32	Jacksonville Jaguars, Carolina Panthers (1995); Houston Texans (2002)
NHL	32	Las Vegas Golden Knights (2017); Seattle Kraken (2021)
NBA	30	Toronto Raptors, Vancouver Grizzlies (1995); Charlotte Bobcats (2004)
MLB	30	Arizona Diamondbacks, Tampa Bay (Devil) Rays (1998)
MLS	30	St. Louis City FC (2023); San Diego FC (2025)

Expansion is practically a cottage industry for North American professional sports leagues. Because existing teams are privately owned, and because new owners are required to pay a franchise fee to join a closed league, it means when league owners vote to expand, those same owners know they are certain to "earn" a multimillion-dollar payout. All for allowing a new owner or syndicate to buy their way into a very restricted "club."

The next time MLS expands, the price tag may approach $1 billion and when that amount is divided by thirty teams, each preexisting owner knows exactly how much they will make (i.e., $33 million-plus on a $1 billion initiation fee [depending on what amount is kept centrally]) for allowing another entrant into their private circle.

In fact, some pundits have suggested the NFL, which requires a controlling club owner who is an individual (not a corporation), is the most exclusive private club in America since there are only thirty-two billionaire members. Still, for a group of private owners to consider expansion requires a series of calculations that can include:

- How much net profit will an owner make for allowing an expansion of the league by one or two new members?

- Will adding a team (or teams) mean the annual distribution of media rights fees will increase or decrease (i.e., $1/32$ of a pooled amount is larger than $1/33$ unless the pie is made larger) from the annual amount received by an existing club?

- Does the new owner and city (where the team will be based) bring incremental value to the collective whole? Will adding a new market potentially grow shared media revenues?

- Does the proposed new owner have the appropriate stadium (i.e., soccer specific with modern amenities) and the sustainable ability to generate acceptable financial returns to visiting teams (the agreed-upon percentage of the gate designated for the visiting team)?

- Will the proposed new owner's personality fit with the existing owners? Are there any political, financial, or social risks to consider?

- Will the new owner potentially bring specific industry expertise (technology, social media, political influence) that helps grow the league and not bring the league into disrepute?

The last two points above always fascinate league watchers who call for expansion because the discussion is more often about the individual and not what a new metropolitan market can bring to the league. Public perception of the new owner (a financially qualified individual capable of paying the league's new franchise fee) and whether that individual "fits" with the community is often misunderstood in the pre-agreement calculus.

Controversial owners are not unknown.

For example, for years, the NFL did not have a franchise in Los Angeles after the Al Davis–owned Raiders moved back to Oakland in 1995. This abrupt relocation denied the NFL fan avidity in America's second-largest media market for the next twenty years before the St. Louis Rams moved to LA for the start of the 2016 season.

On top of two disruptive Davis-led moves (Oakland to LA and LA to Oakland), Davis sued the NFL on numerous occasions generating significant legal costs for the NFL. After his death, Davis's son abandoned Oakland again, this time for Las Vegas.

Other owners, such as Donald Sterling (NBA's Los Angeles Clippers), Daniel Snyder (NFL's Washington Commanders), Marge Schott (MLB's Cincinnati Reds), Malcolm Glazer (EPL's Manchester United), James Dolan (NBA and NHL's New York Knicks/Rangers), Kelly Loeffler (WNBA's Atlanta Dream), and Robert Sarver (NBA and WNBA's Phoenix Suns/Mercury) have all generated significant negative press coverage that various league commissioners were forced to address.

On the positive side of the ledger, adding a team in Los Angeles, when timed with the negotiations for new NFL broadcast contracts, gave the NFL huge leverage with national broadcasters like CBS, NBC, ABC/ESPN, and FOX, as well as X and Amazon. It also brought about the construction of a state-of-the-art new facility in 2020 (SoFi Stadium) and the subsequent relocation of the San Diego Chargers to Los Angeles.

There are other expansion factors to consider as well.

For years, no league wanted to allow an ownership group to operate in Las Vegas because of the widespread presence of casinos and the lingering perception "Sin City" attracted too many shady gamblers.

Then, with brilliant foresight, in 2017, the NHL placed the Golden Knights in Las Vegas. It coincided with changing U.S. opinions (and laws) about sports gambling, and by 2020, the Raiders had moved to Nevada, the Oakland A's announced they would officially relocate (in 2028), and the NBA was signaling it wanted a team in Vegas sooner than later.

Similarly, when the Seattle SuperSonics moved to Oklahoma City in 2008, it meant the NBA no longer featured a basketball team based in the eighteenth largest U.S. market, nor a team in one of the most technologically dynamic cities in North America (for additional insight on Seattle, check out chapter 13).

A side distraction emerged when numerous media critics suggested Oklahoma City was too small for a league that had previously moved NBA teams out of Fort Wayne, Syracuse, Cincinnati, Buffalo, Baltimore, Kansas City, San Diego, Vancouver, and East Rutherford (New Jersey).

Expansion and the prospect of failed expansion make landing on a league's optimal number of teams extremely relevant and challenging.

In Europe, where there are five major football (soccer) leagues, each with fewer teams than any North American league (see chart below), the concept of promotion and relegation eliminates (for all practical purposes) the need for expansion since two to three "new" teams move up every year, thus changing the look of a league. These new clubs are thrust into the spotlight and, in many cases, served up as cannon fodder for stronger, better-financed teams.

Nonetheless, the new arrivals enjoy the media rights benefits denied clubs playing in second level competition. They also fight to avoid getting relegated back down to the league they just left, with huge financial and brand consequences possible from relegation.

European League	Year Started	No. of Teams	Last Teams Promoted (2024)	Last Teams Relegated (2024)
EPL*	1992	20**	Leicester City Ipswich Town Southampton	Burnley Luton Town Sheffield United
Serie A	1929	20	Parma Como Venezia	Frosinone Sassuolo Salernitana
Bundesliga	1962	18	FC St. Pauli Holstein Kiel	FC Köln Darmstadt 98
LaLiga	1929	20	Leganés Real Valladolid Espanyol	Almería Granada Cádiz
Ligue 1	1932	18***	Auxerre Saint-Etienne Angers	Metz Clermont Foot Lorient

*The EPL was created in 1992 as a grouping of the top English teams that separated from the English Football League, a competition that had started in 1888.

**The EPL was composed of twenty-two teams when it launched in 1992 as the FA Premier League (or FA Carling Premiership) but dropped to twenty clubs for the 1995–1996 season when only two clubs (Middlesbrough and Bolton Wanderers) were promoted.

***France's Ligue 1 reduced the number of teams competing from twenty to eighteen for the 2023–2024 season.

What's also notable is that fewer teams in the top European competition means fewer players on active rosters. That reality ensures that only the very best players are seen on the pitch.

By contrast, when expansion takes place in North America, there's a palpable sense the overall increase in the quantity of players competing at the highest level will create a "watered-down" product, as talent is dispersed.

A final component when discussing MLS expansion is whether the eighteen-team premier Mexican soccer league (Liga MX) might ever falter financially or some of its top teams (i.e., Monterrey, Toluca, Club América, Guadalajara, Pachuca) would ever seek to break from Liga MX and petition to join MLS.

Such a move, unlikely in 2025 and perhaps ever, would be subject to massive lobbying, followed by difficult-to-obtain approvals from CONCACAF (and FIFA). Further, with exciting prospects, such an expansion would make MLS a three-country league.

To be clear, it's unlikely MLS would ever suggest expansion into Mexico for a host of reasons including that CONCACAF would not want (nor allow) an American/Canadian league to cannibalize or weaken an important global league operating inside the confederation's boundaries. As it is, North America's massive footprint (versus the much smaller geography of England, France, Germany, Italy, or Spain) means MLS players fly much greater distances for games than their European peers.

This travel reality is rarely discussed as an issue for existing North American leagues, especially when the NFL (England, Germany, Brazil), NBA (Mexico, France), NHL (Sweden, Finland, Czech Republic), and MLB (South Korea, Mexico, England) annually play regular season games on foreign continents while also crisscrossing the sizable North American landmass.

Nonetheless, with technological advances creating increased streaming/marketing efficiencies and making all pro leagues subject to financial sustainability challenges, MLS benefits from economies of scale (provided by a host of major media markets) that other world leagues cannot generate. It partially explains why, as more young North American fans discover MLS and its star players, that expansion for MLS will appear attractive.

Will MLS expand to thirty-two teams by 2028? The odds would suggest it is more than possible. Especially when mega-events such as the 2025 FIFA Club World Cup (officially the Mundial de Clubes FIFA 25), the 2025 CONCACAF Gold Cup, the 2026 World Cup, and the LA 2028 Summer Olympics and Paralympics will drive increased awareness for soccer in North America. There is also the reality that motivated cities and cashed-up investors will make cases they want MLS to consider them and can afford the projected $1 billion needed.

For existing MLS owners, while the due diligence required is often onerous, the upside of expansion might suggest the likelihood MLS gets to thirty-two teams before the decade ends.

There has been a steady rise in MLS expansion fees, and those distributions helped offset the operating losses by clubs. Arthur Blank was awarded a team in 2014 in Atlanta for $70 million, while Minnesota cost $100 million the following year. Nashville (2017), Cincinnati (2018), and Austin (2019) all paid $150 million, while St. Louis cost $200 million in 2019.

David Tepper raised the bar with a $325 million fee for a franchise in Charlotte in 2019. Unlike the previous four expansion teams, the Charlotte Panthers owner did not have to fund a new stadium with a ready-made home at Bank of America Stadium, which he also owns.

San Diego FC joined the league in 2025, after paying a record $500 million fee. Egyptian billionaire Mohamed Mansour is the lead owner and will pay the expansion fee over multiple years, resulting in a net present value of between $400 million and $450 million, depending on the discount rate applied. Mansour is also on the hook for San Diego FC's start-up costs and a new training facility.

Say this much, MLS continues to have success with its newest clubs. St. Louis City SC started play in 2023 and was an instant hit on and off the field. It broke the record for wins by an expansion team on route to the Western Conference title. The stadium was sold out for the season, and the club established a season ticket waiting list. Only Inter Miami, with Leo Messi, had higher merchandise sales.

The last nine expansion teams have all built loyal followings, and among those clubs, LAFC, Atlanta United, Inter Miami, and Austin rank among the six most valuable franchises. Austin has sold out every game since it started play in 2021 and now has a paid season ticket waiting list of twenty-six thousand fans. LAFC, St. Louis, and a resurgent Philadelphia were the other MLS teams to sell out every game in 2023.

One issue MLS needs to solve involves several of its legacy clubs in attractive markets, including New England, Colorado, San Jose, and Chicago. They all sit at the bottom of the financial table but should be in the top half. Those franchises started play more than twenty-five years ago when MLS typically targeted families for its season ticket base.

The more recent crop of expansion teams have built followings among millennials and supporters groups that have created a community around those teams and juiced revenues; new soccer-specific stadiums have also helped. Meanwhile, New England and Chicago have been trying to solve their stadium issues for years.

Expansion teams being worth more than most established teams is not unique to MLS. The Vegas Golden Knights hit the ice for their first season in 2017 and have built a huge following and are valued at $1.3 billion, No. 11 in the NHL. The Seattle Kraken started play in 2021 and rank nineteenth in *Sportico*'s NHL team valuations at $1.12 billion.

The NWSL fetched $53 million for each of two recent expansion teams in Boston and the Bay Area. Private equity giant Sixth Street was the lead investor in Bay FC and expected to invest $125 million in the club, including the expansion fee and start-up costs. *Sportico* values only five of the current twelve NWSL teams above the $53 million expansion mark. In 2023, the Chicago Red Stars sold for $35.5 million.

On the hardwood, the NBA is likely to launch an expansion process soon with Las Vegas the leading candidate among a group of attractive markets. Some owners are floating a $5 billion price tag for a new team.

Twelve new MLS teams have started play since 2015, and San Diego FC is the thirtieth franchise (in total). MLS critics point to teams' reliance on those rising expansion fees as a revenue stream. There is likely room and an appetite for another MLS team or two.

Las Vegas was targeted for an expansion team before San Diego got the nod. Vegas presents a challenge due to the upfront costs beyond the expansion fee. A new venue would almost certainly be the most expensive soccer-specific stadium ever built because of the need for a roof. Phoenix, Charlotte, Louisville, and Indianapolis are all strong possibilities as well.

Interestingly, no major U.S. sports league has ventured past thirty-two teams. The expansion fee spigot will turn off soon for MLS and that means the league will have to rely on their local economics and league growth via the Leagues Cup, the Apple agreement, and other MLS initiatives.

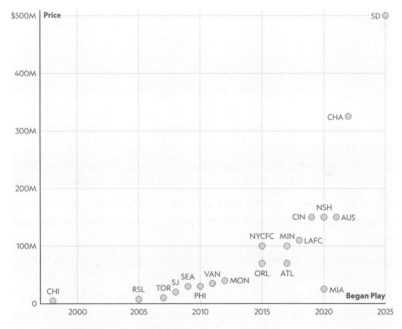

Inter Miami fee in 2020 is the result of an option David Beckham received to buy an expansion team at a set price when he joined the Los Angeles Galaxy in 2007.

Chart courtesy of *Sportico*.

Chapter Nine

COPA 2024, FIFA Club World Cup 2025, FIFA World Cup 2026, and the LA 2028 Summer Olympics

What They Will Mean to MLS

There is no question big sporting events power the global sports ecosystem. They sell tickets in massive quantities, entice advertisers to buy commercial time, and drive ratings for the networks that hold the exclusive broadcast rights.

The annual NFL Super Bowl, MLB's World Series, NHL's Stanley Cup, NBA Finals, MLS Cup, Indy 500, NASCAR's Daytona 500, Masters, and U.S. Opens (tennis and golf) are critically important to those properties, their owners, network partners, sponsors, and merchandising licensees.

In quadrennial systems (events held once every four years), the IOC's Summer and Winter Olympics/Paralympics, the FIFA's Men's and Women's World Cups, and rugby's Men's and Women's World Cup add huge relevance to the sport landscape and consistently generate massive international viewing audiences.

Domestically, the NFL's regular season serves as a gargantuan money-maker for the league, but it's the annual Super Bowl that lifts the NFL into the financial and media visibility stratosphere. This winner-take-all February game has become so big it is practically a national holiday in the United States. It is similar in Canada, where there is not an NFL franchise. Advertising for the game sells out long in advance of the hyped showdown between the American and National Conference champions, and the net haul from advertising revenue is always a record for the host broadcaster.

In the 1950s and 1960s (before the advent of the first Super Bowl in 1967), the biggest tentpole in sports belonged to baseball's World Series. This was a time when portable televisions were wheeled into elementary school classrooms and midweek daytime games were shown to millions of schoolchildren.

The World Series was an American touchstone and the best-of-seven championship always guaranteed at least four contests and, on eleven occasions during those two decades, the Series went the full seven games (1952, 1955, 1956, 1957, 1958, 1960, 1962, 1964, 1965, 1967, and 1968).

What makes these mega-events so important are the residual benefits created by the *reach* of the authorized broadcasters and the *frequency* with which people (word of mouth) and advertisers promote the event. For sports fans, the *R & F* of these extravaganzas are culturally important because they provide a dynamic social currency tied to the competition.

Fans want to know who will win and which superstar is likely to emerge as the MVP. Those questions become conversation starters in almost every setting (including schools, corporate offices, bars, churches, temples, and mosques).

As MLS fans know, the league has its own annual championship but during the five-year stretch between 2024 and 2028, MLS will benefit from six international events guaranteed to collectively elevate the importance of global-style football and MLS, North America's primary soccer league.

The first two already took place during 2024 when the United States hosted the forty-eighth edition of the Copa América men's soccer championship at fourteen U.S. stadiums during June and July of that year. It was immediately followed when Paris welcomed the 2024 Summer Olympics, with Spain taking gold (over France) in the men's tournament. The United States (over Brazil) won the women's gold medal.

The third and fourth are scheduled for the North American summer of 2025 when thirty-two club teams from six confederations play sixty-three games between June 15 and July 13 in the FIFA Club World Cup at eastern U.S. stadiums, including many of the 2026 World Cup host venues. The Seattle Sounders and Inter Miami will be two of the thirty-two participants. Seattle won the 2022 CONCACAF Champions League, and Miami captured the 2024 Supporters' Shield. Similarly, major clubs Chelsea, Al Hilal, Real Madrid, Manchester City, Bayern Munich, Paris Saint-Germain, Inter Milan, Boca Juniors, Borussia Dortmund, Juventus, and Atletico Madrid will be participating.

Overlapping that FIFA club tournament and played in fourteen western North American stadiums (thirteen in the United States and one in Canada) is the 2025 CONCACAF Gold Cup. The final will be hosted in Houston in July. Combined, these two major events should create a groundswell of soccer narratives and growing anticipation in advance of the coming World Cup.

The fifth happens just under a year later when FIFA's 2026 Men's World Cup is hosted by the United States, Mexico, and Canada. The sixth and final soccer mega event will take place during the Olympic Football Tournament at the Los Angeles 2028 Summer Olympics, when gold medals will be presented to the best men's and women's teams.

In the case of the South American Football Confederation's quadrennial 2024 Copa América, the North American Confederation (CONCACAF) was chosen to co-host the event with CONMEBOL as a means of further promoting FIFA's 2026 World Cup. As such, fourteen U.S. host cities (charged with "Rocking the Continent"), produced games in the following venerated stadiums:

- AT&T Stadium—Arlington, Texas
- Levi's Stadium—Santa Clara, California
- Mercedes-Benz Stadium—Atlanta, Georgia
- Q2 Stadium—Austin, Texas
- MetLife Stadium—East Rutherford, New Jersey
- Bank of America Stadium—Charlotte, North Carolina

- NRG Stadium—Houston, Texas
- Hard Rock Stadium—Miami Gardens, Florida
- Arrowhead Stadium—Kansas City, Missouri
- SoFi Stadium—Inglewood, California
- Children's Mercy Park—Kansas City, Kansas
- State Farm Stadium—Glendale, Arizona
- Allegiant Stadium—Las Vegas/Paradise, Nevada
- Inter&Co Stadium—Orlando, Florida

Spread over a one-month period (June 20–July 14, 2024), sixteen teams from the North and South American confederations battled to replace Argentina as the reigning champions from the pandemic-delayed 2021 Copa. Ultimately, Argentina defeated Colombia to retain the title before a sold-out crowd at Hard Rock Stadium in Miami, by a score of 1-0. The highly anticipated game was delayed more than an hour as fans rushed the gates and disrupted security.

While the Copa games did not feature MLS teams, forty-one MLS players populated 2024 Copa América rosters, the second most represented soccer league just behind EPL at forty-two, and ahead of Brasileirao (thirty-six), Liga MX (thirty-five), La Liga (twenty-five), Serie A (twenty), Primera Division (Argentina) (sixteen), Primera Liga (Portugal) (thirteen), Ligue 1 (twelve), and Bundesliga (six). More importantly, local, regional, national, and international media followed the thirty-two-game tournament closely with Fox Sports handling the coverage in North America alongside TSN (English) and RDS (French) in Canada.

What North Americans saw were some of the best players in the world representing countries such as Argentina, Brazil, Mexico, Uruguay, Colombia, Chile, and Costa Rica. In this way, North Americans unfamiliar with elite football heard others talking about the teams who reached the quarterfinals, semis, or finals.

Copa América was not and is not the NFL's Super Bowl but in the world of soccer it was a major tournament conveniently setting the table for the 2025 FIFA Club Cup and 2026 FIFA World Cup. It also provided further media coverage for global football with game results and storylines dominating that summer's sports programming.

The 2026 FIFA World Cup will follow Copa América by less than twenty-four months and where Copa was held in only one country, FIFA wisely provided joint hosting responsibilities to three (United States, Canada, and Mexico) in order to generate unprecedented attention to soccer in North America.

For the World Cup, sixteen cities will play host to the 2026 games, with eleven in the United States, two in Canada, and three in Mexico. The host city list includes:

- United States: Atlanta, Boston, Dallas, Houston, Kansas City, Los Angeles, Miami, New York/New Jersey, Philadelphia, San Francisco, Seattle
- Canada: Toronto, Vancouver
- Mexico: Guadalajara, Mexico City, Monterrey

For many around the world, the World Cup is a "stop what you are doing" event capturing and captivating imaginations for the month the games are played. In numerous countries, regardless of the game's start time (middle of the night, early morning, etc.), diehards will designate public places to meet and then build their personal schedules around watching favorite teams or key games.

The festivities for the 2026 Men's World Cup will kick off on June 11, 2026, in two Mexican stadiums (Mexico City and Zapopan/Guadalajara) with the Mexican National Team playing in the tournament opener in the capital. By July 19, 104 games will have been played with the championship taking place at MetLife Stadium (East Rutherford, New Jersey) just across the Hudson River from New York City.

The 2026 Men's World Cup will be the first year the FIFA country pool expands to forty-eight teams (up from thirty-two), meaning sixteen additional countries will bring their enthusiasm and hopes to North America. The Cup will also feature forty more games than the previous World Cup and a change to the second-round qualifying format. The expansion of teams and format alteration are the first since 1998.

There are some other notable firsts as well.

Cup '26 will be the first ever hosted by three countries and also the first time Canada will host World Cup games. Interestingly, Mexico hosted the World Cup in 1970 and 1986 and with the tournament opener in 2024, emerges as the first country to ever host (or co-host) three World Cups. In addition, the great 87,500-seat Estadio Azteca (which sits at 7,200 feet above sea level) has been given the honor of opening Cup '26 (with Mexico playing in that game). Notably, Estadio Azteca is the only venue to have ever hosted two FIFA World Cup finals.

As for the Olympic football games played in Paris (2024) and Los Angeles (2028), it is important to make clear how men's Olympic soccer is conducted with roster restrictions (all team members must be under twenty-three with three permitted exceptions) and is generally not as prominent in North American broadcasts as swimming, gymnastics, athletics (track and field), or basketball. In this way, the men's tournament, unlike the women's Olympic football championship, is seen by many purists as slightly compromised.

Where no roster restrictions exist for the women's gold medal, winning the women's Olympic football gold medal is often viewed as similar to winning a FIFA World Cup, a confederation championship, or a league trophy.

Despite the limited rosters for the men at LA 2028, the names of many young North Americans playing on the U.S., Mexican, or Canadian national teams will be known by MLS fans and they will hope the best under-twenty-three players are coming to MLS (or are already on MLS rosters).

The 2028 football in Los Angeles will represent the sixth time North America will have hosted Summer Olympics football (St. Louis, 1904; Mexico City, 1968; Montreal, 1976; Los Angeles, 1984; Atlanta, 1996; and Los Angeles, 2028).

How much will these mega events help MLS? One way to investigate this question is by listing MLS cities/teams that are certain to see an upside drawn from hosting any of the five North American-based mega-events: Copa América 2024, FIFA's 2025 Club World Cup, the 2025 CONCACAF Gold Cup, the FIFA 2026 World Cup, or the Los Angeles 2028 Summer Olympics in their home markets.

MLS Teams as Major Event Hosts

City (MLS Teams)	Copa América '24 Games	World Cup '26 Games	2028 Olympics	2025 CONCACAF Gold Cup	2025 FIFA Club World Cup
Arlington (FC Dallas)	Yes	Yes	No	No	No
Atlanta (United FC)	Yes	Yes	No	No	Yes
Austin (FC)	Yes	No	No	Yes	No
Boston (Revolution)	No	Yes	No	No	No
Charlotte (FC)	Yes	No	No	No	Yes
Cincinnati (FC Cincinnati)	No	No	No	No	Yes
Houston (Dynamo FC)	Yes	Yes	No	Yes	No
Kansas City (Sporting)	Yes	No	No	No	No
Los Angeles (Galaxy & FC)	Yes	Yes	Yes	Yes	Yes
Miami (Inter CF)	Yes	Yes	No	No	Yes
Minnesota (United FC)	No	No	No	Yes	No
Nashville (SC)	No	No	No	No	Yes
NYC (FC & Red Bulls)	Yes	Yes	No	No	Yes
Orlando (City SC)	Yes	No	No	No	Yes
Philadelphia (Union)	No	Yes	No	No	Yes
San Diego (FC)	No	No	No	Yes	No
SF/San Jose (Earthquakes)	Yes	Yes	No	Yes	No
Seattle (Sounders FC)	No	Yes	No	No	Yes
St. Louis (City SC)	No	No	No	Yes	No
Toronto (FC)	No	Yes	No	No	No
Vancouver (Whitecaps FC)	No	Yes	No	Yes	No

In all, more than two-thirds (twenty-two) of MLS's thirty teams will benefit from the immediate presence of five massive spectacles staged in their metropolitan TV markets. The LA Galaxy and FC will receive all five, and six others (Atlanta United FC, New York City FC, NYC Red Bulls, Houston Dynamo FC, San Jose Earthquakes, and Inter Miami FC) will receive three.

This visibility for European football is not insignificant and, like other peripheral benefits (think *Ted Lasso*, *Welcome to Wrexham*, and the Netflix drama *The Beautiful Game*), MLS marketers will find a loud buzz continuing to grow as each of the six global men's soccer mega events are staged and discussed.

Further, as MLS technology advances during the 2025–2028 window (see chapter 13), including the possible introduction of 5G technology, generative artificial intelligence, statistical/data manipulation and virtual reality applications/devices, MLS fan engagement, and instant connectivity to favorite teams and players will only grow.

This means a team supporter will be able to follow their favorite MLS player, regardless of where they are from or which national team they compete on. That access will continue increasing in synch with Gordon Moore's famous "Law" that suggested a technological doubling of computing capacity every two years.

Borrowing from that thinking, it's certain MLS fans will enjoy significant growth in technology at a time when football/soccer will take the main stage during the four years spanning summer 2024 and summer 2028.

EXPERT PERSPECTIVE: JOHNNY MISLEY, CEO ONTARIO SOCCER

As CEO of Canada's largest provincial sport organization (soccer), I am continually focused on many aspects of the game. I am also in a province that has more than 15 million people and is home to an MLS club—Toronto FC (TFC)—and hosts many Canadian men's and women's national team international matches. My role requires me to pay attention to sport participation, the development of young talent, driving high performance, all while ensuring we operate as a sound and sustainable business.

Founded in 1901, Ontario Soccer develops and delivers exceptional and sustainable programs and services throughout Ontario with the mission of providing leadership and support for the advancement of soccer in collaboration and cooperation with our member District Associations, partners, and other stakeholders. Ontario Soccer owns and operates the Zanchin Automotive Soccer Centre in Vaughan, Ontario, as well as operating the Ontario Player Development League (OPDL), the province's premier standards-based youth development program, as well as "Team Ontario," Ontario Soccer's provincial Xcel program.

The overall objective of Ontario Soccer as a hub for coach, match official, and player development is to be innovators and leaders in sport and to assist with the equitable development of soccer as a healthy lifestyle choice, provide a talented pathway for participants to excel and encourage inclusive community involvement at all levels.

When I think about our relationship with TFC, numerous things come to mind, including:

1. The TFC Academy—at Ontario Soccer, we seek to create opportunities for young male players to develop from grassroots programs into higher levels of the game such as the TFC Academy. We are the primary supplier of youth talent to the Academy.

2. TFC MLS club—Having an MLS club in our province creates benefits for Ontario Soccer. These include both commercial and player development benefits. Commercially, TFC is one of five Premier Partners providing sponsorship dollars that help supports the development and promotion of the game at the grassroots level. As a development partner, the TFC Academy provides a professional program to further hone the skills of Ontario's top youth age players both on and off the pitch as well as having their teams compete in our Ontario Player Development League (OPDL).

3. Marketing the Game Together—our success equals TFC's success and vice versa. As a result, we work closely together on promoting soccer participation in Ontario to engage Ontarians in all communities.

In addition, the major soccer events coming to North America between 2024 and 2028, some in our province, will impact Ontario Soccer. They include:

1. COPA 2024—although no games will be held in Canada, it is coming to North America and Lionel Messi played in it. For us, it is akin to royalty or a pop sensation arriving in our province and community. Messi is a global brand, is an ambassador for the "beautiful game," and drives public interest beyond the sport of soccer.

2. FIFA Club World Cup 2025—For us, it's another global showcase to proudly witness Ontario representation on Canada's national teams and a salute to a development system we have worked hard for the past ten to fifteen years in development and refining. Now a high majority of players on Canada men's and women's national teams are born and developed in Ontario.

3. FIFA World Cup 2026, including matches held in Ontario. Beyond the pride as stated above, this event is massive in scale, reach, and legacy. It's a once in a lifetime opportunity for all of us in Ontario Soccer to take advantage of and celebrate the game. We can also convert those inspired to register to play, coach, officiate, or volunteer.

4. CONCACAF Gold Cup—also not in Canada, but in the United States. For Ontario Soccer, it is yet another milestone event to showcase Ontario players on our national team against the top competition in the confederation.

5. LA 2028 Summer Olympics—It's one of the pinnacle events for soccer and specifically for our women's national team. Canada's Women's Team were defending gold medal winners heading into the 2024 Paris Olympics. LA 2028 will be no different and most likely draw even more attention being closer to home.

Of these five, for me, the 2026 FIFA World Cup will be incredibly meaningful. Here's why:

1. A Global Audience—The 110 matches are like hosting 110 Super Bowls. There is no greater worldwide audience than the FIFA Men's World Cup. Therefore, attention on our sport pre-, during, and post-World Cup will showcase the sport (and Toronto) above all others for a period of approximately six months.

2. Economic Impact—For Toronto and Ontario? Massive!

3. Legacy—As was experienced by our American friends with the 1994 World Cup, soccer in Canada will benefit post event with a number of legacy pieces such as: growing the sport, growing facility infra-structure, growing revenues through

new business opportunities, growing the profile of the sport, and so on.

Finally, a few words on the future of the sport of soccer in Ontario. I see my country as a NEW CANADA after the World Cup 2026 has been played. Soccer's player representation looks like Canada: very multicultural and very diverse. The 2026 World Cup will ignite and propel the game within Canada's sport ecosystem and, in time, make soccer "Canada's game."

EXPERT PERSPECTIVE: STEVEN MANDIS, AUTHOR
What Impact Will the 2026 FIFA World Cup Have on MLS?

The 2026 FIFA World Cup is the supercharger event for MLS that builds upon Inter Miami signing Lionel Messi in 2023 and the United States having hosted the 2024 Copa América. Those two get followed by the near-simultaneous 2025 FIFA Club World Cup (Eastern U.S.) and 2025 CONCACAF Gold Cup (on the U.S. West Coast). Wow. For that reason, I will focus on the impact to talent and commercial revenues.

Talent

Regarding talent, let me provide some context. Soccer was actually the second major sport, after baseball, to organize professionally in the United States. The United States had reached the semifinals in the inaugural FIFA World Cup in Uruguay in 1930. However, even though soccer had been played in the United States for over a century, soccer was only of nominal concern to most Americans in the 1980s.

Soccer was the preferred sport of many European and South American immigrants. As such, the sport struggled to find the mainstream acceptance that baseball and football enjoyed.

However, when the United States qualified for the 1990 FIFA World Cup (around eight to twelve years after ten- to twelve-year-old American kids saw Pelé and other soccer superstars in the North American Soccer League in the mid to late 1970s), the game in the United States regained some traction.

Before qualifying for the 1990 World Cup, by way of an automatic qualification, the United States hadn't qualified for a FIFA World Cup since 1950. But on July 4, 1988, FIFA awarded the United States, in a narrow 10–7 vote over soccer-power Brazil, the hosting rights to the 1994 World Cup, which meant the United States was "in."

While U.S. soccer joined FIFA in 1913 and Brazil had entered in 1923, there was some initial controversy about awarding the World Cup to a country that no longer had a professional league. The North American Soccer League (NASL), established in 1968, folded following the 1984 season. Therefore, one condition FIFA imposed was the creation of a professional soccer league. MLS was founded in 1993 and the ten-team league began operating in 1996 backed with some deep-pocketed investors such as Phillip Anschutz, Lamar Hunt, and Robert Kraft operating teams.

In preparation for the 1994 FIFA World Cup and without a major domestic professional league, many USMNT players were paid to train all year round together at a national team training center in Mission Viejo, California, south of Los Angeles, for almost two years leading up to the World Cup. In comparison, the 1980 U.S. Men's Olympic Hockey team trained together for seven months.

Most of those at the USMNT training center were not skilled or experienced enough to get good opportunities to play in European leagues. Some of the players like Alexi Lalas and Cobi Jones had never played Cup-level soccer. Out of necessity at the time, they went from college straight to being full-time international players.

At the 1994 FIFA World Cup the USMNT would advance out of the Group Stage—which was an incredible accomplishment.

The USMNT lost 1–0 to Brazil, the eventual winner, in the knock-out round of sixteen, a very respectable score line—especially considering the gap in talent.

While many USMNT players were extremely popular, most never were signed to play in the top five leagues (England, Spain, Germany, Italy, and France) at any point. Of the twenty-two players on the 1994 USMNT World Cup team, only ten would compete in the top five during their careers, which had almost a hundred teams in the 1990s and only four of the twenty-two played more than two hundred games (~five seasons). In comparison, of the twenty players on the 1980 Men's U.S. Olympic Hockey Team, thirteen played in the NHL, which had over twenty teams in the 1980s, and five played more than four hundred games (~ five seasons).

It was the following generations of talent that's interesting.

The number and minutes of USMNT players in the top five leagues increased gradually over the course of the 1990s and early 2000s from not a single player, and therefore zero minutes at the 1990 World Cup to six players and 12,312 minutes in 2006. Those figures then almost doubled in 2010 to twelve players and 23,265 minutes, leveled off in 2014 (small decline) with ten players and just over 23,000 minutes, then dropped sharply in 2017, with only four players playing a total of 9,156 minutes.

The decline surprised me. I discovered there was a talent boom eight to twelve years after the 1994 World Cup reaching a peak in 2006 to 2010—similar to the boom resulting from Pelé's presence in the NASL in the mid-1970s.

Still, the decline from the peak in 2006 to 2010 was more than expected. When the USMNT lost to Trinidad and Tobago in 2017, the number and minutes of USMNT players in the top five leagues (four players, 9,156 minutes) had regressed to less than the 1998 USMNT World Cup numbers (five players, 11,025 minutes). The American players who were inspired by the 1994 FIFA World Cup had aged and were no longer in peak performance.

Number of Players and Minutes of United States Men's National Team in Top Five Leagues

	1990	1994	1998	2002	2006	2010	2014	2018	2022
World Cup Finish	Group Stage	Round of 16	Group Stage	Quarter Finals	Group Stage	Round of 16	Round of 16	Did Not Qualify	Round of 16
World Cup Place	23	14	32	8	25	12	15	40	14
Coach	Bob Gansler	Bora Milutinović	Steve Sampson	Bruce Arena	Bruce Arena	Bob Bradley	Jürgen Kinsmann	Bruce Arena	Gregg Berhalter
Total Team Caps	454	425	1,156	1,153	1,030	813	820	1,245	685
Players in Top 5 Leagues	0	1	5	8	6	12	10	4	12
Percent of Team in Top 5 Leagues	0%	4%	19%	31%	23%	46%	38%	15%	46%
Total Minutes Top 5 Leagues	0	1,857	11,025	12,652	12,312	23,265	23,042	9,156	
Total Minutes Top 5 Leagues (excluding goalies)	0	1,857	6,975	7.972	8,668	15,285	16,359	9,156	
Average Minutes/Player (Top 5)	0	1,857	2,205	1,582	2,052	1,939	2,304	2,289	
Number of Players in Europe	4	6	6	12	12	17	12	5	17
Total Minutes in Europe		7,484	13,674	21,548	31,875	32,140	27,457	13,476	
Percent of Team in Europe	18%	27%	26%	52%	52%	74%	52%	22%	74%
Players in Champions League/Europa League Play	0	0	2	0	1	3	2	1	5
Total Minutes in Champions League/Europa League Play	0	0	750	0	0	1,152	252	546	

Similar to the period after the 1994 World Cup in the United States, I expect a talent boom eight to twelve years after the 2026 World Cup which, combined with a "Messi effect" and new economic incentives to identify and develop players in MLS Youth Academies, will help give the USMNT the talent to emerge as a consistent contender in future FIFA World Cups (recognizing that there are ups and downs and cycles for various reasons).

Many young talented players on the USMNT are expected to be playing in or have played in MLS or be graduates of MLS youth academies. The 2026 FIFA World Cup will also introduce soccer in the United States to foreign superstars thinking of where to play next and MLS's presence will resonate with them.

Commercial Revenues

Academic research shows that commercial revenues have the highest correlation to winning—this makes sense as clubs with more revenues have more money to spend on talent. And one of the biggest impacts of the 2026 World Cup on MLS will be an increase in MLS commercial revenues. However, this was not true in the past.

For historical context, the total attendance and average attendance per game at the 1994 World Cup set records that still hold today, higher than the 2006 World Cup in Germany and the 2014 World Cup in Brazil. The 1994 World Cup was a springboard for the USMNT and the sport in America. The USSF was left with a $50 million surplus after the tournament. Approximately $5 million was used as seed money to launch MLS.

Regarding commercial revenues, I want to provide some context to show how far MLS has really come. By 1998, the USSF, the players, and fans had very quickly forgotten about the enormous strides soccer in the United States had made in less than ten years.

Unfortunately, the enthusiasm from the 1994 World Cup didn't carry over four years later. The 1998 World Cup was shown live on TV in the United States and treated as a major sporting event. However, ESPN ratings dipped about 50 percent overall from 1994.

Encouraged by the TV audience in 1994, ABC rescheduled its popular daytime soap opera *General Hospital* to televise the 1998 USMNT match live against Germany. Unfortunately for MLS, the game had lower ratings than a typical *General Hospital* show and was considerably worse than any USMNT match in 1994.

Worse still, in the 1998 FIFA World Cup, the USMNT finished dead last in the standings, having scored only one goal in three losses. The poor ratings and dismal performance brought with it serious consequences.

For one, Street and Smith's *Sports Business Daily* reported that the 2002 and 2006 World Cups came very close to not being televised in English in the United States. No major networks had bid on the rights.

While the key MLS owners were facing stagnating attendance and staggering losses (MLS had reportedly lost an estimated $250 million during its first five years), they ingeniously (and courageously) formed a subsidiary to buy the TV rights from FIFA, cover the production costs, and ensure the World Cups aired on ESPN. This act played a significant role in the continued promotion of soccer in America. Then MLS leaders negotiated an agreement with ABC and ESPN to broadcast the tournament.

Following 9/11, the three principal MLS owners considered shutting down MLS and even spoke to bankruptcy lawyers. A couple of days later, they changed their minds and banded together deciding to eliminate two teams and keep ten clubs between the three of them. It was a big financial risk. Fortunately, the gamble paid off handsomely and will be further extended by the 2026 FIFA World Cup.

It's worth noting that the United States is the biggest sports market and a key part of growth of soccer/football. In 2018, the United States accounted for 32.5 percent share of the global sports market valued at $471 billion, with the others in the top five being China (12.5 percent), Japan (4.6 percent), Germany (4.1 percent), and France (3.2 percent).

UEFA president Aleksander Čeferin said, "Football [soccer] is extremely popular in United States these days. Americans are willing to pay this amount [gestures high with hand] for the best and nothing for the less. So, they will follow European football as basketball lovers in Europe follow NBA. It's a very important promising market for the future. The thing is that we are selling rights very well."

The increase in MLS expansion rights has been driven by increasing commercial revenues. The 2026 FIFA World Cup is the supercharger event for MLS that builds upon the "Messi effect" for MLS.

MLS is propelling itself into the forefront of sports fans' minds, with more than two million viewers for its biggest matches.[1] The 2023 season was a transformational year as the league set a single season attendance record with 10.8 million spectators attending matches throughout the year, up nearly 9 percent over the 2022 season. In 2024, the league passed the 11 million mark.

MLS reaped the benefits of increased exposure that resulted in a 16 percent surge in sponsorship deals this season. The average number of sponsorships per team rose from sixty-five to seventy-five, with over half of the teams registering double-digit increases in deals.

The surge in MLS's team sponsorship revenue to over half a billion dollars is a remarkable testament to the league's rising prominence and their ability to leverage the global excitement of the World Cup, Lionel Messi's star power, and the Apple partnership.

Additionally, it's important to remember the league's investment in aggressive club expansion (nine markets added in seven years) has been pivotal at driving fan engagement and revenue growth. These factors underscore MLS's growing influence in the global sports landscape, making it an exhilarating time for soccer in North America.

The 2026 FIFA World Cup will only add to the momentum.

---

1. https://frontofficesports.com/2022-mls-cup-viewership/

CHAPTER TEN

MLS

The Diversity Advantage

DIVERSITY IS ARGUABLY THE MOST IMPORTANT AND CONTROVERSIAL consideration in modern human resources, with governments mandating it, organizations seeking it, and academics researching it. It has developed into a broader and more holistic construct—sometimes dubbed diversity, equity, inclusion, and accessibility (DEIA)—based on the well-researched premise that more diverse groups of people make better decisions and produce better results.

That logic is pretty straightforward: a more expansive set of viewpoints, backgrounds, and experiences leads to an improved understanding of a situation, better background knowledge on topics, and a more open view of decision consequences.

When we think of a professional sport league, the DEIA aspect takes two pathways, the on-the-field and off-the-field, with the difference characterized by the fact that the on-the-field aspects are clearly displayed for all who watch or follow. Conversely, the off-the-field (e.g., ownership, team/league administrators) is not something the typical fan or viewer sees regularly.

MLS PLAYER COUNTRY OF ORIGIN
A review of the backgrounds of MLS players finds representatives from numerous countries from all corners of the globe. Both a pre-pandemic (2017) and recent post-pandemic (2023) report by MLS showed

diversity in detail and made obvious the increasingly global nature of the league's player cohort.

The 2023 review of MLS players found eighty-one countries from six continents were evident on MLS rosters. The 2017 and 2023 studies found similar results. Each indicated MLS was (and remains) the most diverse league in North America, with players whose listed birthplaces came from seventy-five countries in 2017, eighty-two in 2022, and eighty-one in 2023. By contrast, in 2010, the country-of-origin number was only sixty.

MLS is also attracting an increasingly strong group of top-notch international players. Beckham, Messi, and Ibrahimović are among the best known, but an avid MLS fan knows world-class players increasingly enter MLS with impressive résumés. Per the 2017 study, many MLS players had been capped by their national teams (38.2 percent) and about 7 percent had participated in a FIFA World Cup. An impressive number of American (sixty-nine) and Canadian (twenty-one) players held national team experience.

In just the six years between the two studies, the trend of a more diverse player base continued. In 2023, the most represented countries, after the United States and Canada, were—in order of number of players—Argentina (thirty-seven), Brazil (thirty-six), Columbia (thirty-two), and France (twenty), all considerable increases over 2017.

Other countries with at least ten players in MLS—in either 2017 or 2023—included England, Ghana, Brazil, Costa Rica, Jamaica, Mexico, Venezuela, and Uruguay.

Many think the NBA is the most diverse and global of leagues, but it trails MLS considerably. This 2017 study reported the NBA had 21.7 percent of its players born outside of the United States and Canada, with a total of forty-five countries represented.

The 2023 data showed the NBA still at forty-five countries and thus much lower than MLS's eighty-one. MLB, also very international in its player composition, sat at 28.7 percent foreign born with twenty-three additional countries represented by its players, about a quarter of MLS's total.

In considering players in Europe's premier leagues, MLS has the most countries represented outside of its two host countries according to the league's 2024 demographic report.[1] At seventy-nine, MLS led EPL (sixty-nine), Ligue 1 (sixty-eight), Serie A (sixty-five), La Liga (sixty), and Bundesliga (fifty-four), as well as the NBA (forty-five), NFL (twenty-nine), MLB (twenty-three), and NHL (twenty-two). Further, only two of the top global leagues had a higher percentage of players born domestically than MLS, led by La Liga (59.5 percent) and Bundesliga (54.1 percent), with MLS reporting that 48.5 percent of 2024 roster spots were held by 332 U.S.-born and forty-four Canada-born players, or 48.5 percent of the overall player pool.

MLS Player Racial Diversity

In 2023, MLS undertook a deep review of their racial and gender diversity across the league, covering ownership, front office management, coaching, administration, sport services, game officials, and players. The detailed report showcased a league making progress to be seen as even more racially diverse and gender equal. More importantly, the mere fact the document was developed and shared publicly is indicative of a league committed to this agenda.

Organizations that benchmark are typically willing to install actions intent on reaching stated benchmarks. As a bottom line, this approach typically leads to positive action.

In the report, which was critical of the League's diversity at the ownership and senior administration level, but positive on most other fronts, some important facts about MLS players were shared. The report gives a grade of A+ on player diversity, well deserved given 61.9 percent of players were reported to be "people of color." Just under one third of players identified as Hispanic or Latino (32.3 percent). The most represented group was white (38.1 percent). Black players made up 24.9 percent of MLS rosters with Asian players (0.8 percent), Hawaiian/Pacific Islander (0.3 percent), and American Indian or Alaskan Natives (0.1 percent) following.

---

1. https://www.mlssoccer.com/news/mls-features-the-most-geographically-representative-and
-youngest-rosters-in-north-american-men-s-sports

Indicative of North America's ever diversifying population, those players who identified as being two or more races increased to 3.4 percent of MLS players, an increase of 0.6 percent vs. 2021.

Looking back to 1999, the first year MLS undertook such a report, a much different mosaic of players was evident with the majority being white (65 percent), followed by Black (18 percent), Hispanic or Latino (16 percent), Asian (0 percent), and Other (1 percent), all much lower than 2023 levels.

Admittedly, there are more clubs and more players, and the world is much different than when it waited for Y2K to arrive. But, even considering league expansion, the per capita change is so significant the diversity point is clear.

LOCAL DIVERSITY ALSO MATTERS

This chapter easily focused on the global reach of MLS, but equally important for any sport league is its local market and linkages to the people who might purchase season tickets, a suite, or a single game ticket. The notion of the "local hero" is essential to this argument, where the inclusion of a player from a local market, even if they are not a key part of your team. For example, in the NBA, if your twelfth player—who would rarely play—is a hometown player, research shows, the club will benefit financially.

Thus, as important as it has been for MLS to attract global stars from many countries, it has also been as key to bring in U.S. and Canadian players. In the United States, California, a long-time hotbed of soccer, led the way in MLS representation with, as of 2023, sixty-one players.

The province of Ontario, Canada's leading soccer producer, had twenty-five MLS players, three less than the second most-represented U.S. state of New York and three ahead of the third most-represented state, Florida.

A star player is important to any club, in part, because fans will buy the replica jersey of someone they wish to discuss about over coffee each morning. Every team has a star (or stars) at the local level, but very few feature global stars like Beckham, Ronaldo, Mbappé, Kane, Haaland, or

Messi. These special few drive revenues, but the majority of club-level stars do not drive much incremental revenue.

Since few MLS teams attract global stars, most do well to build up regional stars. If a team wants to grow revenues via player acquisition, the next best approach may be a domestic or local hero strategy. Of course, and this does matter, a team will not want to undermine the success of the club by selecting a player who might cost more and contribute less (or both) than the best available talent at a given position.

But within the confines of that limitation, if a player (be it the backup goalkeeper or one of the substitutes for defensive purposes) can be selected who will not hurt club performance on the field but who provides a strong local link for the club, they should be considered or even possibly sought out.

A player born in the club's city, or who grew up there, or who represents a key portion of the population, or who played college or developmental level soccer there. The examples are many for MLS teams such as an Italian national linking to a city's significant Italian population. Or a hometown prodigy who went away to play in Europe but returns triumphantly.

DIVERSITY OF PLAYERS: SHOULD ANYONE CARE?

A case can be made that MLS is one the most diverse, in terms of players. Period. But one might ask, why does this matter? How does this aid in the league's off-the-field success?

Well, there are a number of reasons, certainly logic, and some academic support for this fact. Indeed, one study on the NBA and the "racial congruency" of its audiences with the composition of its teams, found that the better a team represented its local market, the better it did financially. In short, linking a team and its players to the market is important.

As an example, here is the most recent census of the United States (2021) and Canada (2020), as noted in this table.

Ethnic Background	U.S. Census	Canada Census
White	57.8%	67.6%
Asian	6.1%	18.7%
Indigenous	0.7%	4.8%
Black	12.1%	4.2%
Multiracial/Other	4.6%	3.1%
Latin American	18.7%	1.6%
Total	100%	100%

*Note: a few assumptions made by the authors regarding groupings

In the table above, both countries reflect a white majority but are becoming increasingly diverse and are expected to be less than 50 percent white by 2045 (United States) and 2050 (Canada). Additionally, for both countries, the larger urban areas, where professional teams play, will be far are more diverse than suburban and rural areas.

The Brookings Institution,[2] in reflecting on the 2020 U.S. census, described the results as a "diversity explosion" in general but with diversification happening in different ways in different parts of the country. The reports noted that in 95 percent of U.S. counties, the proportion of the population that identifies as white declined between 2010 and 2020.

The fastest-growing racial and ethnic groups were Latino/Hispanic, Asian, and those with two or more races. Maps of the country broken down by representation depict a country where groups are highly represented in certain areas but not others: Black Americans were predominant in the south; Latino/Hispanic Americans in the west, Asian Americans in Texas and other specific areas, and Native Americans in Oklahoma. At the city level, there were also cities with a predominance of certain groups such as Asian in Seattle, Black in Atlanta, Latino/Hispanic in Los Angeles, and white in Pittsburgh.

Another important trend in the United States and Canada is the aging white population combined with (or offset by) a growing diverse younger population. The largely white baby boomer population is

2. https://www.brookings.edu/articles/mapping-americas-diversity-with-the-2020-census/

entering its retirement years, while the highly diverse Millennials and Generation Z cohorts, who are more predisposed to soccer, are entering the workforce and gaining discretionary income.

This "cultural generation gap"—a combination of age and ethnicity/race differences—is a new and powerful trend that aids MLS and soccer, the world's most popular and diverse sport. As of 2019, in the United States, more than half of the under-sixteen population identified as a racial or ethnic minority. This trend was fueled by both increasing interracial marriages (about one in five new marriages in the United States today are between couples from different racial backgrounds, according to the Pew Institute) and increasing immigration to the country, with immigration accounting for 74 percent of Asian American growth and 24 percent of Latino or Hispanic growth in the decade leading up to 2020.

In Canada, the 2021 census[3] revealed similar trends toward ethnic diversity, particularly in younger populations, with racialized groups growing and concentrated in certain areas (e.g., Black in the province of Ontario and Asian in British Columbia). Almost 80 percent of immigrants to Canada report a high level of importance on their origins, a supportive point for soccer.

The fact the Canadian census found more than one third (35.5 percent) of the Canadian population reported two or more countries of origins further supports this. For example, more than 2 percent of the Quebec population (or about 170,000 people) identified as "Italian" by origin, most of whom live in the Greater Montreal area, home to CF Montréal.

In Canada, according to census data, between 2016 and 2021, the proportion of the population that identified as South Asian, Chinese, and Black went from 13.6 percent to 16.1 percent, or 5.8 million people. This number is expected to exceed 11 million by 2041.

Finally, much like the United States, most of Canada's immigrant population (69.3 percent) in 2021 were from countries and cultures where soccer is important. For example, Toronto is home to the largest South Asian, Chinese, Black, Filipino, West Asian, Latin American, Southeast Asian, and Korean populations in Canada.

---

3. https://www150.statcan.gc.ca/n1/daily-quotidien/221026/dq221026b-eng.htm

ANALYZING MLS PLAYERS PAST AND PRESENT

An MLS database revealed that 3,811 MLS players, current and former, had played games in MLS as of the end of 2023. This represents all (or almost all) of the players who have played in the league since its launch. The data set included the player's country of origin, name, season they started in MLS, year they finished, and how many total games they played.

Of the 3,811 players, the statistics revealed the players represented 126 different countries, averaged 3.58 seasons and 58.58 games played in MLS. On average, MLS players participated in 15.8 games per season over the league's history. The longest career length is 22 years and the most games played was 514.

Players from the United States (n=1,487) played the most games, followed by players from Canada (143), Argentina (191), the United Kingdom (168), and Brazil (158), which represented the top five of the 126 countries.

In total, this set of players played 147,109 MLS games, an astonishing number, until one considers there are only twenty-two players on the field during any game. Interestingly, nearly four thousand players averaged almost a sixty-game career each. When considered by country of origin, seventeen countries produced elite athletes with more than one hundred total MLS games played.

Country of Origin	Total MLS Games Played
United States	6,802
Canada	557
Argentina	534
United Kingdom	449
Brazil	443

Colombia	425
France	267
Mexico	248
Jamaica	247
Costa Rica	203
Ghana	192
Honduras	160
Uruguay	154
Spain	128
Venezuela	124
SFR Yugoslavia	111
Trinidad and Tobago	104

Other interesting facts included:

- Of the fifteen players who have played more than seventeen MLS seasons (at least one game), sixteen of the seventeen were Americans.
- For career length, although the average is 3.58 years, the median is only two years, with more than one third of players (34.8 percent) playing just a single season and 53.7 percent playing only two years. Only one-third of players (34.3 percent) achieve a fourth MLS season.

In considering games played, a similar phenomenon is observed with only 18.7 percent of all MLS players, to date, reaching 100 games played and a mere 1.7 percent played in excess of 300 games.

NORTH AMERICA IN 2050: HOW MLS IS POISED FOR THE FUTURE

The recent census results of the United States and Canada provide a picture of two countries experiencing massive demographic change, with younger populations, driven by migration, immigration, and birth rates speeding diversification. This is all highly aligned with the potential for soccer, MLS, and each of its clubs.

Imagining it is 2040, readers will see that citizens who identify as white (or Caucasian) represent minority populations in Canada and the United States. That means North American cities have become microcosms of the world, with populations that are majority non-white, and vast groups of residents from all continents (except Antarctica).

MLS will have already represented that demographic reality for years and will logically continue doing so. In other words, what Americans and Canadians see on MLS pitches (or during MLS streaming) will replicate what they see in their urban communities or what they read in their national census statistics.

CHAPTER ELEVEN

How Toronto Became an MLS Stronghold

FOUR OF THE FIVE MAJOR NORTH AMERICAN SPORTS LEAGUES—NBA, MLB, MLS, and NHL—have a presence in both the United States and Canada. It's only the NFL that doesn't have a franchise in Canada. However, the NFL does operate NFL Canada, which is based in Toronto, and, according to a 2023 study by Angus Reid,[1] the NFL is the second most popular sport in Canada with 20 percent of the adult population following it closely.

The NHL, which is the most popular league in Canada by a wide margin (36 percent of adults follow closely according to that same study), has seven franchises, while MLB and NBA both have one. MLS has three.

That same Angus Reid study found MLS to be the sixth most popular league in Canada with 9 percent, trailing the NHL (36 percent), NFL (20 percent), MLB (19 percent), Canadian Football League (16 percent), and NBA (13 percent).

In 2007, MLS joined NBA and MLS with one club in Canada, with the launch of Toronto FC in Canada's largest city and biggest media market. In following years, clubs in Montreal (the Impact entered in 2012; changing to CF Montréal in 2021) and Vancouver (the Whitecaps joined in 2011) were added to give the MLS the largest proportion of clubs of any major league except the NHL.

---

1. https://angusreid.org/nfl-vs-cfl-grey-cup-vs-super-bowl/

It was Toronto and the success of the Toronto FC, however, that paved the way for MLS expansion into Canada's second and third largest markets.

The same year (2007) David Beckham first suited up in the MLS, the league expanded north when Toronto FC began play. Over its history, the club has featured numerous global stars and achieved notable on-the-field success. Sebastian Giovinco, Jozy Altidore, Michael Bradley, and Jonathan Osorio are some of the former European premier league players.

Toronto FC's Home Advantage

Toronto FC play their home games at BMO Field, on the grounds of the Canadian National Exhibition (CNE). A soccer-specific stadium in the heart of Toronto's largest city, BMO Field is the right size, in the right location, in a great metropolitan city.

Built in 2007, BMO is the fifth sports stadium to be housed on that site and it is easily reachable by foot, bike, or transit. The stadium is owned by the city of Toronto but operated by Maple Leaf Sports & Entertainment (MLSE), the sport entertainment conglomerate that owns Toronto FC, Toronto Maple Leafs, Toronto Raptors, and Toronto Argonauts. The Canadian Soccer Association (Canada Soccer) was a founding partner in the project.

Although BMO Field does allow tenants from other sports, with the CFL's Argonauts starting to play there in 2016, BMO is an example of a "soccer-specific stadium," the style that MLS has championed since the early 2000s. Indeed, it is one of the shining examples of the soccer-specific stadium initiative of the League, with the combination of the MLS club and the role it played in hosting the 2007 FIFA U-20 World Cup as drivers for its funding, which included MLSE as well as federal, provincial, and local government. BMO Field is also home to Canada's men's national team (soccer) and has hosted rugby games on occasion, including the rugby sevens competition during the 2015 Pan-American Games.

Originally built with just more than 21,000 seats, the venue has undergone a few major renovations since being built in 2007. In 2010, natural grass was installed and by 2016, to prepare for the arrival of the

Argonauts and Canadian football, an upper deck was added and the field lengthened. The seating capacity went to 30,991 for soccer and 26,500 for CFL football configuration. With temporary seating, the stadium can handle 40,000 for major events (MLS Cup, the Grey Cup [CFL's championship game]).

BMO Field hosted the Grey Cup in 2016. In 2019, another update to the field surface took place, updating it to a hybrid grass field. With the 2026 FIFA World Cup coming, where BMO Field will host games, a further seating expansion is underway to take seating capacity for BMO Field to 45,736, including a $37 million investment from the city.

EXPERT PERSPECTIVE: IMRAN CHOUDHRY, MANAGING PARTNER OF T1 FUTBOL

A View from Toronto

First off, we're going to have to get one thing straight. It's futbol, not soccer. But just so we don't get North American audiences upset, we'll call it soccer!

Second, let's drop the term *niche sport* from our soccer vocabulary. I hear that too often. Yes, some might call it niche . . . but I've never considered the world's most popular sport, the most played sport, the most watched sport, niche.

Third, I have the unique vantage point of running a soccer specific agency based in Toronto. I see this as a strategic advantage. Toronto is a futbol-loving, I mean, soccer-loving city. We are often referred to as a global melting pot, an incredibly diverse population. Toronto is also a sport mecca. What better place in the world to incubate global soccer marketing campaigns for top brands, properties, leagues, clubs, federations, and anyone else looking to connect with some of the most passionate fans of the beautiful game, than Toronto.

All you have to do is head to a local soccer pitch any day of the week and you'll find games, practices, leagues, pick-up games of friends and/or families spending time together with the only real thing you need to play the game, a ball. Players from under three years old right up to older than you can imagine kicking a ball around. Soccer Canada has more than one million registered soccer players.

Toronto is home to more than 150,000 of those. The most popular team sport among Canadians ages five to fourteen is soccer. And we haven't even started talking about the number of fans of the game. Or how immigration and upcoming immigration targets will continue to impact the growth of the fan base in Toronto. The market is significant and growing, with brands looking to capitalize on the passion point.

Toronto FC

You can't talk about soccer in Toronto, or Canada, without talking about Toronto FC. Since its inception in 2007, soccer in Toronto has experienced remarkable growth. But Toronto has always been a hotbed for soccer passion and soccer talent. Most people don't know the first game of what was called "association football" was played in the city of Toronto back in 1876, or that Toronto hosted Canada's first ever World Cup qualifying match in 1957 with a 5–1 win over the United States.

The long history of soccer in Toronto has created a groundswell of energy riddled with several starts and stops. Then, enter TFC, mixed with a little of that underground fire, and that was all the gas needed to make the city soccer scene blow up. The introduction of Toronto FC brought professional soccer to the forefront of the city's sports scene, igniting excitement among fans and inspiring a new generation of players.

The growth of soccer programming across the city has been and continues to be vast. City run clubs, ethnic based leagues and clubs, academies, supporter (fan) clubs like the Red Patch Boys, and U-Sector all created opportunities for new and seasoned fans to engage with the sport and contribute to the city's soccer culture.

On the field, Toronto FC and some of the club's biggest legends like Dwayne De Rosario, Michael Bradley, Jimmy Brennan, Sebastian Giovinco, Jonathan Osorio, and Jozy Altidore have helped put the city on the map and give fans a reason to cheer. The arrival of TFC has given Toronto soccer fans a reason to watch MLS and the domino effect continues.

MLS in Toronto

Major League Soccer has played a crucial role in the growth of soccer across Canada, including Toronto. Without MLS, there is no TFC. While the league tried some unique things early on that candidly failed (ever watch the penalty shots in early MLS years?!). Overall, the league has been leveling up year after year. As the premier professional soccer league in North America, the success of Canadian MLS clubs has helped popularize the sport and attract more fans and participants nationwide.

If there's one thing North American professional sports leagues know how to do, it's put on a show. MLS has tapped into the right ownership groups who understand the market size and opportunity for growth that soccer provides, creating right-sizes stadiums and engaging the community to further drive passion. And the return on investment is showing with league average attendance steadily increasing since inception and television viewership data also indicating growing interest in MLS, with the league securing lucrative broadcasting deals with major networks such as ESPN, Fox Sports, and TSN/RDS, and now with a landmark deal with AppleTV.

The Growth Drivers

The 1994 FIFA World Cup played a role in promoting soccer in Toronto and Canada as a whole. Despite not being hosted in Toronto, it had a significant impact on soccer in Canada, setting attendance records and generating widespread media coverage.

Given the proximity of the tournament, it allowed Canadian soccer fans easier access in key time zones and lighter travel compared to previous tournaments. It inspired a new generation of fans and kids to take up soccer. The legacy of 1994 included the development of soccer-specific stadiums and infrastructure in the United States, laying the foundation for growth across North America.

This only sparked renewed interest in the sport in Toronto. Similarly, the upcoming 2026 FIFA World Cup is expected to have a profound impact on soccer in Toronto, fostering increased interest, participation, investment, and jobs in the city. With the multicultural mosaic that exits in Toronto, fans will have the opportunity to cheer on their home countries, right on their front step.

I'm sure the team at Toronto FC would love to say they planned the success from start to finish, and the reality is the club did a fantastic job at building up the energy before the club even stepped foot on the pitch. Credit to MLSE (owners of Toronto FC) who saw the opportunity to invest in soccer at a time where the demand that had gone unmet for too long.

From the announcement strategy to the players they signed, the kit design to the investment in a soccer-specific stadium, the working relationship with city officials, and especially the community engagement strategies, Toronto FC head office leveraged their decades of experience with marketing their other sports franchises to maximize the opportunity with Toronto FC with a fan-first centric approach. TFC gained a reputation for having a passionate fan base when it set an MLS attendance record for a standalone match with 20,148 fans attending the inaugural home opener at BMO Field.

One might say they got a bit lucky to be launching the same year David Beckham arrived in the League, and while storylines like Danny Dichio making history scoring Toronto FC's first ever goal and the moments following where home fans littering the field with their souvenir seat cushions could've never been planned, Toronto FC ownership executed against their strategic plan ensuring interest was at a high, including season tickets.

Hosting Canada's Men's National Team matches at BMO Field, or rather the National Soccer Stadium, since 2007 has undoubtedly contributed to the growth of soccer overall in Toronto. These high-profile matches provide fans with opportunities to support their National Team, several of which happen to play for Toronto FC as well.

The opportunity to experience top-level international soccer firsthand fosters a sense of pride and excitement within the community. It has also laid the groundwork for the city and stadium to secure games during the upcoming 2026 FIFA World Cup. This will only help drive further interest in the sport across Toronto with new fans who can easily transition to cheer on a local club after the World Cup tournament.

The 2026 World Cup, 2025 Club World Cup, and 2025 CONCACAF 2025 Gold Cup

It would be impossible for the 2026 FIFA World Cup to not have an impact on the Toronto community at large. In fact, I believe it will have a transformative effect on soccer in the city. The tournament's global reach and magnitude will put Toronto on the world stage, attracting visitors from around the globe and leaving a lasting legacy of increased interest, investment, and infrastructure development in the sport.

While accessibility to watch games live will be a challenge for organizers given the high demand and low inventory of tickets, events surrounding the FIFA World Cup such as the FIFA Fan Festival, pop-up viewing parties, consumers hosting their own watch parties, bars, and restaurants leveraging the games, not to mention the myriad of community events that will be going on, will engage the millions of Torontonians who have been hearing about and waiting for the moment to arrive.

I'm on the fence about how the FIFA Club World Cup in 2025 will impact broader Toronto audiences. Time will tell.

Will Toronto soccer fans get excited? Of course they will. We footballers get excited about everything footy related.

The tournament's prestigious nature and participation of top club teams from around the world will generate excitement and elevate the city's status as a premier soccer destination *if* Toronto FC can show up in an authentic way. Still, I'm not holding my breath.

I think it's yet to be seen if Canada and Toronto FC specifically can leverage CONCACAF events such as the Gold Cup to further increase their fan base. I see a time where fans of Toronto FC may have never lived or even stepped foot in Toronto or seen a Toronto FC match live. I'm a Barça fan yet have never lived in the city or been able to watch "my" team play live.

That's what the greatest clubs around the world have done. They continue to attract a fan base from outside their home territory. Can CONCACAF help Toronto FC do that? Yes, but those clubs had a long head start, so it may take a while!

The Future

There's no doubt in my mind that soccer in Toronto in ten years will still be on its upward trajectory, with continued growth in participation, fan engagement, and investment. The city's diverse population and passionate soccer culture will ensure a vibrant and dynamic soccer scene, with Toronto FC and other local clubs playing a central role in shaping the sport's future. In 2035, Toronto FC will no longer be the only big name in the game though. I see the landscape of MLS changing with more competition from other leagues and clubs in the Toronto area.

The growth of the women's game with Project8 and the growth of the Canadian Premier League, League1, as well as universities in Canada now offering sports scholarships will challenge for the soccer fan's share of wallet.

That said, if MLS and Toronto FC can maintain their position as the top-tier division, continue to engage community stakeholders, as well as put a real emphasis on the player development pathway to ensure more Toronto youth soccer players are achieving their dreams of playing professionally and representing their home city club, then I think Toronto FC valuation today is a fraction of where it will be in 2035.

Toronto's On-Field Success

In its early days, Toronto FC wasn't a high performing on-the-field club. In fact, in its first nine seasons, the club never finished in the top ten in the league, its highest result being eleventh in 2010. Toronto did host the MLS Cup in 2010, but not as a participant, as the host in the days when it was held—like the Super Bowl—went to a neutral site, which was Toronto that year.

It was not until 2015, the club's ninth season, that they did not have a losing percentage since they finished 15–15–4.

Things changed considerably starting in 2016, with the club finishing in the top five three times between 2016 and 2020, earning runner-up status at the MLS Cup in 2016 and 2019, and winning the MLS Cup in 2017.

In 2017, the club won what is known as the "domestic treble," as they took the Canadian Championship and the MLS Supporter's Shield, along with the MLS Cup. The Canadian Championship, organized by Canada Soccer annually, is a pan-Canadian domestic competition involving all professional clubs (from all leagues).

Toronto FC won this championship in 2009, 2010, 2011, 2012, 2016, 2017, 2018, and 2020. The FC were also runners-up in the 2018 CON-CACAF Champions League. Many link the club's success in the 2015 to 2020 period to Tim Leiweke, who was CEO of MLSE from 2013 to

2015, having previously played a key part in David Beckham's 2007 move to the LA Galaxy. Leiweke was the first MLSE leader who had a deep soccer background and made a public commitment to turning TFC into a winning club on the field.

Between 2021 and 2023, five years after Leiweke departed, the club struggled greatly, finishing twenty-sixth, twenty-seventh, and twenty-ninth in MLS those years. Their record for those three years was a dismal 19–56–27. The 2024 season saw the club finish with a mediocre 11 wins against 19 losses and 4 draws.

Toronto FC has fielded a number of teams with top players and global stars. The most successful is Sebastian Giovinco, an Italian player known for scoring goals. He joined the club in 2015 from Juventus, one of the world's most famous clubs, and played four seasons with the club, scoring 68 goals in 114 games. He was sold to a Saudi Arabian club before the 2019 season. Giovinco won the MLS's Golden Boot in 2015 (22 goals in 33 games), the only Toronto player to win that honor. He also had 16 assists that same season, with his total of 38 offensive points setting a new MLS record at the time.

While Giovinco was the most successful player in the history of Toronto FC, Lorenzo Insigne, who as a thirty-year-old signed a four-year contract with the club starting July 1, 2022, is the most famous global player to wear the club's colors, following a sixteen-year career with Italian club Napoli including eleven seasons, debuting at age nineteen, with the Serie A (Italian Premier League) club where he scored 118 goals and won three major titles. He was also a fixture on the Italian National Team, the Azzurri, from 2012 to 2021 with fifty-three caps, nine goals, and being a key part of a European championship win in 2021. Although he scored six goals in ten games for Toronto FC in 2022, he only scored four goals in each of the 2023 and 2024 MLS seasons.

A few other Toronto FC players have won major awards in addition to Giovinco's Golden Boot. Giovinco (2015) and Alejandro Pozuelo (2020) won MLS MVP awards, Maurice Edu was the 2007 MLS Rookie of the Year, Giovinco the MLS Newcomer of the Year in 2015, Greg Vanney MLS and CONCACAF Coach of the Year in 2017, Jozy Altidore was MLS Cup MVP in 2017, Giovinco captured the

CONCACAF Champions League Golden Ball in 2018, and, in that same year, the CONCACAF Champions League Golden Boot went to Jonathan Osorio.

Toronto's Off-Field Success

Off the field, Toronto FC has been an unquestionable success for MLSE, its owners. Its public valuation today is nearly US$700 million, up from a US$10 million expansion fee paid twenty years ago. The club currently has one of the highest payrolls in MLS and its brand (fans call the club TFC or the Reds) has been successful as well.

Support of the club has been strong since the very beginning with the club selling out all home games for its first three seasons when they would draw more than twenty thousand fans per game. Poor on-field performances hurt ticket sales after that, with the club lowering prices in 2013 back to original 2007 levels.

The club has averaged more than 20,000 fans per home game in all its seasons, except for 2012 and 2013, when performance was notably poor, and 2020 and 2021 due to the global COVID-19 pandemic. TFC's highest average crowd was its MLS Cup championship season of 2017 at 27,647 per game and the 2023 season at 25,310 per game.

In terms of the most watched Toronto FC game, that was when the Reds played against the LA Galaxy at Rogers Center (home of MLB's Toronto Blue Jays) in March 2012 in the CONCACAF Champions League quarterfinals.

The highest attendance for a game at BMO Field came in December 2016, when TFC hosted the Seattle Sounders FC in the MLS Cup, losing in front of 36,045 people.

Although MLS reports Toronto FC regularly ranks among the top five of all MLS clubs on many of its business metrics, their ability to draw large television audiences and attract media rights fees has not been strong, but with the growth of MLS's media (and potential revenue sharing) from the Apple deal, this may change. Since 2023, all of the club's matches are streamed on Apple TV via MLS Season Pass, with a few matches concurrently shared on TSN (English) and RDS (French).

Prior to 2023, Toronto FC matches had been shown by CTV and TSN (2017 to 2022), TSN and Rogers Sportsnet (2011 to 2017), and CBC, Sportsnet, and The Score (2007 to 2010).

TORONTO FC ACADEMY

One of the most important achievements of Toronto FC is the club's efforts to grow the sport in Canada, attract youth to the game, and support the development of its club in the long-term. The club invested in youth development at many levels, including a training facility—BMO Training Ground—in the north part of Toronto, and operating, since 2013, the lower-tier club Toronto FC II after launching the Toronto FC Academy in 2008.

The TFC Academy, as it is called, is the youth development arm of the club that works with young players from U12 through to U20 levels. They play out of the BMO Training Ground, which offers year-round training facilities. Owned by MLSE, the venue also has numerous pitches, offices, and other facilities.

EXPERT PERSPECTIVE: TOM ANSELMI, FORMER COO OF MLSE

The "Magical Time" of Toronto

When I think back to the launch of Toronto FC, I remember it as a magical time. It was such a pivotal era in MLS's evolution.

The league launched in 1996 so the context for Toronto is a league that is only ten years old at the time. That created both opportunities and challenges but all of them were very positive. We were attracted to soccer and, specifically, to MLS, for several reasons.

Soccer was the fastest-growing sport in Canada and MLSE were fans of the game and believers in its potential in Canada. The demographics of Toronto were perfect, and the fan base was already there. Toronto is a diverse market and soccer fans in Toronto always went crazy during the World Cup, Euro, and other major soccer events. EPL audiences were strong. Soccer pubs were busy on Saturday mornings. So, we knew the fans were there.

The question was whether they would buy into a domestic league. We got that answer very quickly.

We had done our homework on some of the Toronto pro teams that had failed in the past. They folded for a variety of reasons, but due to things we could overcome. Leagues failed around them. There were cases of under-resourced ownership and overspending on players. These were "running before walking" kinds of issues.

Ultimately, we were convinced MLS and Toronto were positioned perfectly, and the circumstances were ripe for success. As I noted above, though, MLS was only ten years old and still going through growing pains. The average MLS attendance then was about 15,000 per game, but some teams drew well below 10,000, and there were few soccer-specific venues.

There were some examples of success but not many. Still, we felt MLS was clearly going in the right direction. The ownership groups were committed and well resourced. There was solid leadership in the head office and a lot of things were going in the right direction.

The franchise fee was not that significant for a company our size. BMO Field was in play because of its role in hosting games during the 2007 FIFA U20 World Cup.

So, we rolled the dice, and rolled up our collective sleeves.

The Franchise Launch

About a year before launch, we put some of our top people on soccer, hired others with MLS experience, and before you knew it, we were preparing for the 2007 season. The league had a lot going on, and we were the first non-U.S. expansion. That meant there were different rules for Canadian player content, FIFA implications of a cross-border league, a complex money-losing business to understand, and not much time to try and pull it together. But it was exhilarating!

The magic in all of this were Toronto's soccer fans. They embraced the team right from the get-go, and what started as a solid marketing launch quickly became a runaway train led by the best soccer fans in North America. And, wow, did the train leave the station quickly! Our people did a lot of good things, but it was the fans who really took over.

It was something to behold and really, in hindsight now, a pivotal point in the League's evolution and current success. TFC really demonstrated what was possible. We saw the tribal effect of soccer, which is very regional but magnified when it involves national and international brands. All of the things that make soccer really unique around the world were playing out in front of us. Our fans ran with it, and it was amazing to see.

The Power of the Fans

When I say the fans ran with it, I'm referring to 2006–2007, when social media was gaining traction but not nearly as ubiquitous as it is today. But that was the new medium, and everything about the club was happening there. The good, the bad, and the ugly! We didn't spend anything on traditional advertising. It was the first property we marketed almost exclusively on social media.

When the fans took over, it was a tribal thing. They owned it, they posted, they shared. Then, the local fan clubs got engaged. It was something to see, and it really changed MLS. I truly believe that. It led the League's administration to see what was possible.

It led to Montreal, Vancouver, and a handful of teams in the United States as expansion ramped up. When you look at what is going on today, MLS is an important league that sits squarely on the global map. Franchise values have skyrocketed. Players, especially Canadian players, have a league they aspire to reach. Toronto fans have a team of their own, and one that proved it could win a championship.

David Beckham Arrives

We went on sale with tickets in the fall of 2006, and we were doing quite well, exceeding targets, fans were committing, and they were excited about the inaugural season. Then Beckham's signing was announced in January and things just exploded. Tickets sold out, sponsors lined up, and the business took off.

The other interesting part of how the story evolved is MLS's business model. We were attracted to MLS because of its central entity model with a hard salary cap which provided player cost certainty. There was control over player costs. They had a development model that provided a pipeline of the American players coming out of college. It was especially attractive to an expansion franchise and a new business like ours.

All of a sudden, the designated player rule came into play and Beckham's involvement changed things. MLS players that had previously been too expensive were sold. But MLS was now a buyer in the international player market. That changed expectations.

Expansion franchises are notoriously tough enough, so when you're limping along, trying to become a franchise, trying to build culture, trying to create a development system, other variables are changing pretty dramatically.

I'll say this much, it made for an exciting ride! We did a lot of things well, made our share of mistakes, but in hindsight, Toronto now has a team that until Lionel Messi's arrival was the jewel in the MLS crown. We changed the league forever.

What Would We Do Differently?

Hindsight is always 20/20. The business was an award-nominated franchise launch, so not much to change there. There are a lot of little things I'm sure we could have done differently for quicker short-term success on the pitch.

We could have been more aware of MLS's evolution as a league, how players were acquired, especially Canadian players. We could have been more aggressive early in trying to take advantage of the changes in MLS, like investing in designated players, scouting, and coaching. The league evolved very rapidly at the time, ironically, in part, because of our success.

What Were Our Best Business Decisions as a Club?

We made some good decisions early about how to build the brand to be seen as authentic and credible, and we had a real strategic focus on player development for the Canadian system. While those were long-term strategic decisions that didn't necessarily deliver immediate results, they are the foundation of the incredible property that is TFC today.

The Toronto FC brand was well thought out and designed to be authentic so it would be accepted by Toronto (and Canada's) experienced and sophisticated soccer fans. We deliberately chose red, not blue—the classic color of Toronto teams. Red is Canada's color, and we were, at the time, the only MLS club in Canada.

We built the brand to be seen as having soccer credibility. We stayed away from the style of North American team names and conducted a lot of work with soccer fans locally to test names. We wanted to see what the soccer community, ex-players, coaches, and others would embrace. And then, as I wrote above, the fans took it, ran with it, and ultimately defined it.

Another thing we did right was producing a clear focus on the development of the game in Canada and identifying players in Canada for TFC and the Canadian National Team. Sport excellence is a pyramid driven by aspiration. Players in Canada now had something to aspire to and a place to play.

At the time, Canada hadn't made the World Cup since 1986. Canada Soccer was doing what it could to support the national program, but most Canadian players with potential were playing or developing overseas. Young men with talent were heading to academies overseas earlier and earlier. That was part of the strategy right from the start. Keep them home.

Our owners were supportive and made a big investment in the Downsview training facility and the academy. The academy, Toronto FC2 (a lower division professional club), and youth programs were started. We worked with media partners and others on developing nuanced elements of the game such as coaches, TV analysts, medical staff, and trainers.

Those were long-term decisions that took a long time to pay dividends, but now we (MLSE) have a franchise worth twenty-five times what we paid for it. The captain of the team, Jonathan Osario, is a local kid we developed in our system and just one example of our many development successes. We also produced a national team that qualified for the World Cup in 2022 for the first time since 1986.

Most importantly, I feel we're just looking at the tip of the iceberg. Just like the 1996 World Cup in the United States launched MLS, the 2026 World Cup in Canada and the United States will have an enormous impact on the next phase of the evolution of MLS and soccer in North America, especially Canada. To that I say, "Buckle up!"

CHAPTER TWELVE

Ted Lasso, Ryan Reynolds, and EA Sports FC

How Celebrities and Video Games Continue Lifting MLS

How much did *Ted Lasso*, *Welcome to Wrexham*, and a popular video game benefit MLS?

Confidential MLS research probably would reveal significant upticks in data trends starting in 2022 but, at the very least, we know one viable answer is this: Two incredibly popular network streaming shows and a graphically dynamic in-home (or mobile) simulation of MLS competition sure didn't hurt.

The use of sport in popular culture (i.e., live theater, recorded music, books, movies, TV shows, commercial advertisements, and fashion) has existed for more than a century. Sport lends itself to these cultural co-ops because our favorite games produce champions and heroes.

In 1927, Babe Ruth appeared in a silent movie called *Babe Comes Home* where the Yankee slugger played Babe Dugan, the star of a baseball team who chews enormous amounts of tobacco. He also would ultimately generate numerous product endorsements for underwear, chocolates, cigars, chewing tobacco, soda, sporting equipment, and hats.

Given Ruth's massive popularity, it's not surprising during the next century, more than one hundred baseball movies were made and while their intent was always to generate profits for their investors and producers, a major beneficiary of these actions was Major League Baseball.

A selected list of baseball movies that logically benefited Major League Baseball's popularity during the last ninety-five-plus years would likely include the following films:

1. *Casey at the Bat* (released in 1927)

2. *Slide, Kelly, Slide* (1927)

3. *Up the River* (1930)

4. *Elmer, the Great* (1933)

5. *Alibi Ike* (1935)

6. *Pride of the Yankees* (1942)

7. *The Naughty Nineties* (1945)

8. *The Babe Ruth Story* (1948)

9. *The Stratton Story* (1949)

10. *Take Me Out to the Ball Game* (1949)

11. *It Happens Every Spring* (1949)

12. *Kill the Umpire* (1950)

13. *Angels in the Outfield* (1951)

14. *The Pride of St. Louis* (1952)

15. *The Kid from Left Field* (1953)

16. *The Winning Team* (1953)

17. *Fear Strikes Out* (1957)

18. *Damn Yankees* (1958)

19. *Safe at Home* (1962)

20. *Bang the Drum Slowly* (1973)

Numerous other examples of sport infiltrating other entertainment sectors exist including the 1955 Broadway musical *Damn Yankees*; the 1971 TV movie *Brian's Song* (about NFL football players Brian Piccolo and Gale Sayers); NBA star Michael Jordan advertisements for Nike, Gatorade, Chevrolet, Wheaties, and Hanes; numerous basketball and hockey movies; or mainstream rappers wearing hats associated with pro teams (e.g., the Oakland/LA Raiders).

Missing, at least in North America for much of the twentieth century, were movies or television "shout-outs" to European football (soccer). North America had its own sports ecosystem (baseball, football, basketball, ice hockey, circular auto racing tracks) and didn't need sporting codes popular elsewhere (soccer, rugby, cricket, badminton, snooker, Australian rules football, or any number of other Olympic sports where Americans did not perform well).

European football was for Europeans and for the first eighty years of the twentieth century, there were few indicators film producers or advertisers were willing to risk using "soccer" to advance their narratives.

Miller Lite, a rising low-calorie beer brand from Milwaukee, may have been one of the first to test the water when it featured Englishman Rodney Marsh in a 1980 commercial as a break from their steady parade of retired football, baseball, and basketball stars. Marsh had previously played for Fulham, Queens Park Rangers, Manchester City, and, at the time of the commercial, was retired from the NASL Tampa Bay Rowdies.

The following year, actors Sylvester Stallone and Michael Caine appeared in a World War II POW feature film titled *Victory* where Allied soldiers (including Pelé playing a Trinidadian corporal) take on a German team. The 1981 movie, filmed in Hungary, performed better overseas (where it was titled *Escape to Victory*) than it did domestically, but it, too, showed Americans that soccer existed.

Twenty-one years later, at the height of British superstar David Beckham's run through Association football, the movie *Bend It Like Beckham* built on the excitement and charisma of the 1999 FIFA Women's World Cup, concluded notably by Brandi Chastain's successful game-deciding penalty kick at the Rose Bowl in Pasadena. Moments later, when Chastain ripped off her uniform, she revealed she was wearing a sports bra. Conservative America gasped in shock, but the image of Chastain was soon featured on the covers of national magazines such as *Sports Illustrated* (with the single headline word "Yes!"), *Newsweek* ("Girls Rule"), and hundreds of newspapers.

Bend It Like Beckham did not perform particularly well in U.S. movie theaters when it was released in early 2003, but the release of the movie on DVD and video (for either rental or purchase) performed in the top ten for both of those categories. Once again, it seemed women were the beachhead for introducing soccer into the mainstream.

That brings us to *Ted Lasso*, a fictitious comedic character first created as a promotional advertisement by NBC Sports and *Saturday Night Live* cast member Jason Sudeikis to promote NBC's coverage of the English Premier League (EPL). When the promo spots were well received, Sudeikis and others formulated the concept of an American football coach getting hired by the fictional English team AFC Richmond. The premise, in simple, is that Lasso, who knows nothing about European (or Association) football will fail.

Sudeikis's portrayal of Lasso is filled with folksy charm and deliberate humor that, in many ways, reflected North America's unfamiliarity with the EPL or any of the other major European football leagues such as the Serie A, Bundesliga, La Liga, and Ligue 1. Lasso was a bumbler when it came to association football, but his kindness, humility, and team-first orientation played well across the United States and Canada.

When *Ted Lasso* launched on Apple TV+ in August 2020, most Americans were stuck at home trying to evade contracting COVID-19. By the time the series concluded in 2023 (after thirty-four episodes spread over three seasons), it was a regular award winner (Emmys, Golden Globes, Screen Actor's Guild) and held the distinction (from its first year) of being the Emmy Award's most nominated first-season comedy and Apple TV's most watched television series.

Almost overnight, Americans were talking about a type of football that didn't include the NFL. *Ted Lasso* was the "it" TV show everyone needed to watch, and Apple later reported that airing *Lasso* for the second year increased viewership sixfold vs. the initial season. The Lasso phenomenon even went so far as to produce colorful (if not garish) Ted

Lasso merchandise (sold online and at retail) including socks (a six pack of the "Casual Crew") with the polyester/spandex blend marked with familiar terms like "Believe," "Diamond Dogs," and "Be a Goldfish."

Lasso's success may also have caused Apple executives to look at the global potential of an American soccer league, MLS, that had been steadily improving since 1996. The MLS of 2023 was far removed from the league's early years, and while they were not yet paying European-level salaries to their players, North American marketing and communications acumen (on how to better promote "soccer") was growing almost exponentially.

In February 2024, Messi and Sudeikis (playing his Ted Lasso character) appeared together in a Michelob Ultra advertisement during the most watched Super Bowl ever. This unique pairing, along with a cameo from former NFL quarterback Dan Marino, placed soccer on the world's largest stage and showcased MLS's Messi dribbling a soccer ball through a throng of beachgoers.

Messi's foray into beer advertising wasn't his only high-profile appearance. Anyone walking through New York City's Times Square would likely have noticed promotion of Messi's clothing collection of hoodies, T-shirts, and beanies at the Hard Rock Café. And it wasn't just happening in NYC. It was worldwide.

In the above examples, an MLS icon (not to mention one of the game's true GOATs) was featured in two culturally significant settings and indirectly making clear that North America's most prominent soccer league was continuing its highly visible ascension.

The other funny thing was this: Starting in the early 2000s, American millennials (Generations Y and Z) began following European football teams even though they often couldn't watch games live but instead were forced to pick up information or video clips from material posted on the internet. This generational fascination didn't happen overnight, but many North American children were raised playing youth soccer and, consciously or unconsciously, actively taking note of the world's best players.

Suddenly, in high school hallways and across college campuses, students were wearing Manchester United or Real Madrid merchandise. In addition, English Premier League teams began actively pursuing exhibition games in the United States and Canada. In some ways, it seemed like the EPL's biggest teams (United, Liverpool, Arsenal, Manchester City, Tottenham, Chelsea) were signaling they were ready to bring an international sport to one of the most saturated sports markets in the world.

Even Bayern Munich of the Bundesliga opened an office in New York City as a means of promoting the strongest of the German clubs. Meanwhile Real Madrid was inspiring a 2016 book titled *The Real Madrid Way* written by finance and economics professor Steven Mandis of Columbia's Business School.

Clearly, North America's fascination with European football was growing and it eventually led to a monstrously successful 2022 documentary-style series called *Welcome to Wrexham* built around actors Ryan Reynolds and Rob McElhenney buying a small (fifth division) Welsh football club called Wrexham A.F.C.

Numerous reports have suggested McElhenney had fallen in love with a sports documentary series called *Sunderland 'Til I Die* on Netflix. The "you are there" style of the documentary made him want to buy a team and along with Reynolds, they entered discussions with the fan-controlled Wrexham Supporter's Trust in 2020. By February 2021, the popular duo owned the team and immediately started filming content in December 2020, long before the docuseries had even been announced.

Like *Ted Lasso's* character (i.e., an American completely unfamiliar with European football), neither Reynolds nor McElhenney had any experience owning or running a professional sports team. That, of course, made *Welcome to Wrexham* perfect for American audiences still emerging from the episodic viewing (or binging) patterns established during the COVID-19 pandemic of 2020–2021.

Perhaps, not surprisingly, FX (a pay TV channel owned by Disney and available in the United States via Hulu) optioned the rights to the proposed docuseries and began airing episodes in August 2022. Leveraging Disney's ownership of ESPN, Reynolds and McElhenney were promotionally nimble enough to get three Wrexham games aired on ESPN2 and ESPNews during the 2022 season.

While this book doesn't need to describe individual episodes (thus not ruining viewing experiences for anyone wanting to watch well-made football shows), the first two award-winning seasons of *Welcome to Wrexham* benefited from dramatic season ending finales (with significant celebrity cameos) that, had the show been written as a screenplay, Hollywood executives might well have dismissed the entire project as far too imaginative (or unbelievable).

Even better, as *Sportico* reported in late March 2024 (Badenhausen, March 28) Wrexham enjoyed a fantastic fiscal year (ending June 30, 2023) and reported revenue for the club had skyrocketed by +75 percent to $13 million (more than tripling the annual revenues before Reynolds and McElhenney bought the club).

While the increase was driven by merchandise sales (+200%), sponsorships (+79%), and ticket sales (+18%), net losses for the team reached $6.4 million. Perhaps not surprisingly, the two actors did not appear worried since Wrexham had been promoted from England's National League to the Football League (where club revenues were likely to significantly increase again).

Who were the beneficiaries of both *Ted Lasso* and *Welcome to Wrexham*? One short answer is MLS and its teams, largely due to the increased awareness of European football by American audiences.

A second vertical helping the league's growth was the growing appeal of EA Sports's popular soccer/football video game that was called *FIFA* until 2023. Thereafter, it was called *EA Sports FC* with the abbreviated year following (i.e., *EA Sports FC 24*). Perhaps more importantly, from *FIFA 2000* onward, MLS teams and players were included as an option for gamers. Thus, while players in MLS may not have been viewed as the equal of their European peers, the video game/online community was exposed to MLS league and team branding.

It also meant two generations of young American gamers (primarily Gen Y and Z) were exposed to MLS and could start to manage local/regional teams or choose to play "friendlies" against EPL or La Liga giants. EA Sports FC 25 was released in September 2024 with Jude Bellingham on the cover.

This "access" for a growing legion of MLS fans was key. In previous generations, most notably with baby boomers, in-home gaming had involved baseball board games (with dice or spinners) such as Strat-O-Matic, APBA Baseball, or All-Star Baseball or electric football sets or NBC's Pro Playoff (that incorporated preset play-calling cards).

The ability for fans of MLB or the NFL to "manage" or "coach" their favorite real-life teams and players kept those professional leagues top of mind and built in additional avidity for the coming years when those young fans obtained the disposable income to attend professional games in person.

For MLS, the league needed at least ten years from its inception in 1995 before it probably started seeing benefits produced by graphically rich video games displaying the names, images, or likenesses of the league's players. It also meant that when EA Sports lured Lionel Messi away from a competitor (*Pro Evolution Soccer*) in 2012 and placed Messi on the cover of their game for four straight years (*FIFA 13–16*), millions of young American fans became even more familiar with the striker considered one of history's greatest.

That Messi (eight Ballon d'Ors, six European Golden Shoes, FIFA world champion with Argentina in 2022) would join Inter Miami was certainly massively valuable for MLS, especially to global football fans. But to American teenagers and young adults who had been playing *FIFA* since 2012, Messi was not unknown to them. In fact, they already knew his video game abilities but could now start the world's most productive player in Inter Miami's distinctive home pink or away black with pink piping. Even better, they could play as Messi on Xboxes, PlayStations, Windows, and Nintendo Switch.

Notably, of the twelve players selected by EA as representatives of *EA Sports FC 24*'s men's Team of the Year, Messi was selected alongside Manchester City's Erling Haaland and Paris Saint-Germain's Kylian Mbappé as the one of three forwards (Cristiano Ronaldo of Al Nassr, also a forward, was designated the official twelfth player). Still, Messi was the only MLS player given the honor of appearing within the twelve.

This chapter started by asking if two TV series and a popular video game have elevated MLS's appeal. The answer? Who knows?

It's almost certain, though, that *Ted Lasso, Welcome to Wrexham,* and *FIFA 2012–23* (plus *EA Sports FC 24 and 25*) didn't hurt. They contributed, with hundreds of other cultural clues, to a well-orchestrated strategic plan by MLS and team executives to grow the soccer business in North America.

Another example of soccer in the digital world includes Football Manager, a beloved soccer video game launched by Sega in 1992 that today has more than 7 million players. When playing Football Manager, gamers try to become the best soccer coach in the world. This game is frequently monitored on Twitch, and broadcaster Zealand Shannon has done much to popularize it, especially in the United States. Shannon posts daily videos on YouTube in which he discusses any relevant (or irrelevant) news and topics throughout the soccer world; and he cohosts a podcast with Julian Gressel, who played on Messi in Miami during the 2024 season. In the years to come, it's feasible that TV shows and films will annually be created detailing specific MLS teams and players. And while baseball, football, and basketball content won't disappear, it's a safe bet North Americans are about to see more and more MLS content.

CHAPTER THIRTEEN

Tech Cities, Tech Teams, Tech Stadiums

How Technology Is Reshaping MLS's Relevance

THERE IS AN OLD SAYING THAT CLEVERLY SUGGESTS IF GLOBAL CITIES are not getting smarter, they must, by logic, be getting dumber or falling behind. There is no standing still. That concept may seem unkind or, perhaps, something a normal person would never stop to think about. Cities are cities. They just exist.

Or do they? Are some cities smarter than others? Can a city get smarter?

Are some cities better at conducting business or attracting national conventions and huge sporting events? Do certain metropolitan areas have better infrastructure incorporating artificial intelligence and powerful wireless networks (not to mention security safeguards) keeping citizens safe and public transportation humming?

Is it possible some cities are just more fun and vibrant than others? Do they have a well-known downtown district with a national reputation for great bars and restaurants?

The answers to all of the above, as evidenced by tourism dollars, tax revenue, and economic vitality, is "yes." Some metropolitan areas are aggressive about their future. Others, for a variety of reasons, are not.

Certainly, New Orleans, Nashville, Fort Lauderdale, or Daytona Beach are well known for their historic encouragement of visitors (and implied promise of "good times").

Lists created by various media outlets confirm this and it partially explains why the ranking of American cities is relatively common. The variables used may vary (livability, economic growth, "great places to live") but eventually a website or print magazine like *Business Insider*, *Daily Beast*, *Forbes*, or *Outside* gets around to assessing the levels of education a city holds, the amount of technology it uses for infrastructure, or access to mountain bike trails, whitewater rafting, and spectacular hikes.

One publication, *Sports Business Journal*, even rates the best sports business cities when it comes to event hosting. In their 2024 ranking (*SBJ*, March 18–24, 2024), *Sports Business Journal* tabbed Orlando as the "most successful at attracting and hosting sporting events" and thus creating "economic drivers" for that Florida market.

Right behind Orlando in *SBJ*'s annual Top Ten were Las Vegas, Los Angeles, Atlanta, Indianapolis, Arlington (Texas), New York City, Houston, Phoenix, and Columbus (Ohio). But *SBJ* didn't just rank big cities. They included special sections on "Cities Without a Big Five Team" (won by Forth Worth, Texas) and "Ones to Watch" (topped by Austin, Texas, where MLS's Austin FC are the only Big Five team).

Annual rankings generally change over time, but public perception is usually a strong indicator when it comes to determining whether a city holds the "it" factor. In fact, it's not uncommon for sports fans to think a certain city is where everyone is going.

Take Las Vegas for example.

It undoubtedly surged in the *SBJ* rankings by hosting the 2024 Super Bowl and by securing an annual Formula 1 race there in 2023. It also doesn't hurt that what was once known as "Sin City" (due to its wealth of world class casinos/hotels) has, within the last ten years, added the Las Vegas Golden Knights (NHL) and Las Vegas Raiders (NFL) and will add MLB's Athletics (from Oakland) as early as 2028 as well as an NBA team before the decade ends. The NBA tipped their hand recently by concluding their first two in-season tournament championships, the NBA Cup, in Vegas at the end of 2023 and 2024.

Las Vegas is also home to the Ultimate Fighting Championship (UFC) headquarters and fighter training facility, the National Finals Rodeo (NFR), as well as the University of Nevada, Las Vegas (UNLV) which competes in the NCAA's Mountain West Conference. In other words, almost overnight, Las Vegas has emerged as one of the biggest North American sports cities, and it won't surprise MLS fans if Vegas is given an MLS expansion team post 2025.

The Los Angeles geo footprint or "zone" is another great example (as far as big cities go).

Southern California not only features ten Big Five teams (Dodgers, Angels, Lakers, Clippers, Rams, Chargers, Kings, Ducks, LAFC, and Galaxy), but will also host key games for the FIFA 2026 World Cup before hosting the International Olympic Committee's 2028 Summer Olympics. It will also undoubtedly host major pre-Olympic events in 2027 (prior to 2028) as well as games for the 2031 Men's Rugby World Cup and 2033 Women's Rugby World Cup.

That's a snapshot of two sports cities.

When it comes to "smarts," though, a different set of variables will influence rankings. Here, certain cities regularly earn ongoing accolades.

Boston traditionally does well on "smart city" lists because it is home to influential research institutions such as Harvard, MIT, Tufts, Boston College, Northeastern, Emerson, and other settings of higher learning.

Seattle and San Francisco traditionally score well because major companies like Amazon, Microsoft, Google, Apple, Meta, and Intel are housed there and consistently hire professional employees pushing the technology envelope. The same can be said for North Carolina's Research Triangle (featuring the University of North Carolina, Duke, and North Carolina State); Austin, Texas; and Vancouver, British Columbia.

A third type of city ranking is one where "adequate public safety, emergency response and other critical services while prioritizing energy resilience" (Britt, *Forbes*, 2023) are valued. These cities may feature modern airports, reliable public transportation, and a strong, trusted police presence.

The above is a long way of writing that in looking at cities, readers might determine some are better than others (based on unscientific ranking criteria). The same holds for sports leagues where fans will rationalize some teams are better than others at ticket sales, fan engagement, customer promotions, sponsorships, or technology.

Asked about the MLS universe, Chris Schlosser, the senior vice president for Emerging Ventures at MLS, suggested numerous variables continue to shape how the league's teams are rated when discussing technology and the enhancement of the fan experience in a team's stadium. Schlosser noted the use of phones to present game tickets or as a directional tool (i.e., locations of fastest gate entry, concession stands with the shortest lines), but he also referenced overall venue connectivity (which warrants continual wi-fi upgrades) as important initiatives.

In addition, regardless of the team or stadium, every MLS match is streamed via MLS Season Pass which allows fans to use the Catch-Up function, the Condensed Game, or Quick Highlights feature. This benefits not only fans who can't attend games involving their favorite team (or those of others they follow secondarily), but also fans who rush home from attending a game to get a different look at the action just viewed from their stadium seat.

"Teams are really leaning into game data," said Schlosser in a 2024 interview, "and generating game-based tracking details on every player. There's a lot of *Moneyball* activity going on. But we are also one of the most advanced 'stats' leagues in the world and that's driving the presence of coaches on the sidelines with iPads checking individual performance. Our fans want those statistics as well."

Schlosser made clear MLS was one of the first football/soccer leagues in the world to roll out Video Assisted Referee (VAR) in a non-intrusive way. The League also built a VAR Center in Texas for monitoring every single game and will undoubtedly investigate automated offsides technology in the future through the possible use of microchips in match balls.

Asked about specific MLS teams, Schlosser acknowledged St. Louis City SC was very tech forward from the very beginning and had developed one of the league's best club apps that helps manage every part of a city fan's experience with the team. The St. Louis approach to innovation was notable enough that *Sports Business Journal* created a four-page profile of this MLS team for their November 27, 2023, issue.

"The [St. Louis] stadium, designed by HOK and Snow Kreilich," wrote Bret McCormick, "reflects a club that knew to localize the venue in every way possible, starting with food and drink. When St. Louis

City asked fans to suggest local restaurants to consider including in the stadium's F&B program, it received 10,000 submissions from the public."

Cutting-edge technology for the building was also paramount.

"The stadium is truly post-pandemic; it's never accepted a paper dollar or ticket. The club [also] took advantage by incorporating more fan experience tech into CityPark's original design," including self-checkout and checkout-free technologies, "as well as a mobile-heavy F&B ordering system backed by MLS's only in-house app development team."

As noted in *SBJ*, St. Louis City (at the time) was the only MLS team "with its team business offices, training facility, team store, and stadium located in a contiguous 31-acre setting amid a major city, all of which are connected to the same fiber internet network." It was also the only stadium in professional sports offering loge boxes where animals could have ticketed seats (a courteous nod of the head to sponsor Purina which is headquartered in St. Louis).

One final area worth noting, specifically as it relates to teams and their technical connectivity to fans, is the tech savviness of key players. There are few football players (of any style such as NFL, AFL, or international rugby) to match the appeal and following enjoyed by Messi. At one point during 2024, Messi had amassed more than 500 million followers on Instagram.

In this way, Inter Miami was the beneficiary of Messi's worldwide appeal. Beyond what the team produced for their website or posted on social media it was Messi's frequent digital deliveries that created the most visibility for his home club.

"We're glad Lionel Messi, the best player of all time, chose to continue his career in MLS," Camilo Durana, MLS's EVP of Apple partnerships, properties and events, said in an email to a reporter at *Sportico*. "While we're certainly focused on the opportunities that come with Messi, we're equally focused on making sure new fans fall in love with the incredible clubs, players, supporters and communities that make MLS what it is" (Pelit, 2024).

That same article made clear Messi's presence had caused subscriptions to "MLS's Season Pass on Apple TV [to] more than double since

Messi's arrival, and Spanish language viewership on MLS Season Pass on Apple TV [had] surpassed over 50% [of all viewers] for his matches."

According to MLS, Inter Miami's first 2024 "preseason game against El Salvador, where Messi played the first half of the match, generated the most single-day traffic in MLSSoccer.com's history with 49 percent of viewership on the site in Spanish via MLSes.com. The preseason match was [also] broadcast on the league's website instead of MLS Season Pass."

There is no question MLS matters greatly to its fans and players. And it is that growing legion of supporters who have made MLS a full member of the Big Five North American professional sports leagues. That achievement, unimaginable to many sport traditionalists as recently as 2015, bodes well for MLS's future.

Further, because MLS has embraced technology, the league will continue operating as a global giant providing its international fan base with meaningful games, highlights, and stories on a 24/7/365 basis.

As this book is published in 2025, MLS will have kicked off a new season and expanded to thirty teams (adding San Diego FC), and the commissioner will have made clear to team executives they must meet their fans and casual observers where they live: on digital devices that fans carry with them and check all the time.

Additionally, where the league has publicly stated it intends to reach thirty-two teams sooner than later, it will also make the necessary investments to keep pace with the inventions sitting just around the corner. Those "disrupters" may include virtual reality opportunities, holographic proximity to star players, artificial intelligence customizing products, data to fit specific fan interests, and increased benefits at tech-savvy stadiums.

It's probably safe suggesting MLS fans won't be surprised when a future magazine or website ranks the top twenty most technologically advanced sports teams or stadiums, and MLS clubs or venues heavily populate that list.

EXPERT PERSPECTIVE: JARROD DILLON, PRESIDENT OF BUSINESS OPERATIONS FOR ORLANDO CITY SC

As the Sports and Entertainment industry continues to evolve, how to reinvent your venue has continued to be a competitive space for clubs with existing tenured venues. Teams and venue operators alike are constantly evaluating how they can improve their facilities and provide the best experience possible for their fans and attendees.

In Orlando, Florida, under Wilf family ownership since the summer of 2021, the Orlando Pride (NWSL) and Orlando City (MLS) soccer clubs have seen a tremendous amount of investment into their business growth. From 2021 to 2023, Orlando City paid tickets increased 46 percent, and Orlando Pride paid tickets increased 71 percent.

Combined corporate partnerships grew by 30 percent during that time period as well. In addition to MLS and National Women Soccer League matches, their twenty-five-thousand-seat downtown soccer specific stadium has hosted many events such as Copa América, SheBelieves Cup, U.S. men and women's national team matches, and many international friendlies with the likes of Arsenal, Flamengo, Aston Villa, Fulham, River Plate, among others.

While looking for ways to reinvent their stadium and deliver the best guest experience possible, the clubs had a great opportunity coming into 2024 with a new naming rights partnership, while also celebrating their tenth season in Major League Soccer.

On January 18, 2024, the clubs announced a new landmark ten-year naming rights partnership for INTER&Co Stadium. This partnership marked the first ever Latin America–headquartered company to secure naming rights of a U.S. sports venue. Through this partnership club ownership and the executive team were able to significantly enhance and reinvent their stadium fan experience.

INTER&Co Stadium's "Orlando Made" food/beverage program, in partnership with Oak View Group, has quickly become a fan favorite and point of differentiation in the marketplace. The initiative has been focused on providing stadium attendees with local flavors and brands. The program now includes over twenty local food and beverage brands available in-stadium to fans, while allowing operations to see a significant upturn in speed of service, sales, and fan satisfaction.

In partnership with Amazon and Fanatics, INTER&Co Stadium became the first soccer-specific stadium in North America to deploy Amazon's Just Walk Out technology at their team merchandise store, breaking the club's record for highest net revenue at a single match for Orlando City's 2024 MLS home opener. With Amazon's Just Walk Out technology, fans are able to spend less time checking out and more time enjoying the action on the pitch. Guests enter the store, take what they like, and leave by using RFID (Radio Frequency Identification) tags in their clothing and other apparel.

INTER&Co Stadium was upgraded to Wi-Fi 6 and 6E, the fastest and most up-to-date technology available. Additionally, 5G antennas were installed throughout the venue to offer increased cell phone coverage for those attending events.

Fans are now treated to a best-in-class experience through the newly upgraded INTER&Co Stadium 60' × 34' videoboard, located in the southeast corner of the bowl. The videoboard is complemented by over 150 feet of new LED fascia signage, totaling over five million new LED pixels to create an immersive experience for fans. Additionally, a new 16' × 9' LED wall in the West Club provides all fans with the ability to continue watching the match while taking advantage of the space's complimentary food and beverage. The LED wall is also utilized to enhance private events at the venue.

Acting on feedback from fans, the club invested in more than 230 new televisions throughout INTER&Co Stadium, including upgrades to the venue's premium areas, and throughout the concourse and at concession stands so fans can keep an eye on the action from anywhere in the venue. On the concourse outside the West Club lobby, the new digital Jersey History Experience presented by Orlando Health allows fans to look back at the most iconic jerseys from Orlando City and Orlando Pride history. The interactive display showcases the Club's kits, while providing insight and education on the stories that made each one so special.

Along the concourse fans can also find a new Selfie Station, where they can immortalize their visit to the venue and take a photo next to a digital version of their favorite Orlando City or Orlando Pride player.

The Orlando Pride and Orlando City SC intend to continue setting the bar for fan experience and in welcoming fans to the enhanced and reimagined INTER&Co Stadium for years to come. Vamos Orlando!

Chapter Fourteen

Predicting MLS's Future

A book about the rise of MLS would be incomplete unless it also attempted to predict where MLS is headed. The league in 2025 will look completely different by 2035. It's going to get bigger, better, and more global. It is going to grow in revenues, profits, fans, and player quality.

To be sure, the successful execution of COPA 2024, followed by the CONCACAF 2025 Gold Cup, the FIFA 2025 Club World Cup, the FIFA 2026 World Cup, and the IOC's Los Angeles 2028 Summer Olympics will all raise soccer's profile in North America.

So will the growth of the women's professional game (NWSL) and the continued expansion of the game globally which will influence the consumption habits of America's and Canada's ever-diversifying population. As Apple technology delivers MLS games into Asia, the Middle East, Oceania, or any soccer-loving corner of the globe, MLS will flourish.

In addition, as individual MLS teams view the success enjoyed by Inter Miami during 2023 to 2025, due in large part to the presence of Messi, it is logical to suggest Messi won't be the last great player to view MLS as a high-quality league capable of generating sold-out stadiums plus lucrative salaries and endorsement deals.

In fact, it remains possible that players like Ronaldo, Mbappe, Martinez, De Bruyne, Bellingham, Kane, Haaland, and Salah may sign with, or at least consider joining, an MLS club during their careers.

In three short years with Inter Miami, Messi showed he could sign or keep agreements with savvy brands such as Apple TV, adidas, Budweiser (which includes Michelob Ultra), Cirque Du Soleil, Gatorade, Hard Rock, Konami, Lays, Lowe's, Mastercard, Mengniu, Ooredoo, ORCAN, Pepsi, Royal Caribbean, Saudi Arabia Tourism, Socios, Sorare, YPF, and others. Not surprisingly, with each passing week, it has seemed like a new brand in a different category was adding the Argentine star to their marketing programs.

To wit, if Messi represents a "rising tide" for MLS players, it should also suggest many MLS team "boats" will float higher. Not only that, but as MLS welcomed San Diego FC in 2025, rumors will remain ripe MLS intends to reach thirty-two teams before 2028.

This calculated expansion, if achieved, will generate incremental visibility for the league and set off two more regional waves of marketing, public relations, and fan engagement. It is also possible MLS will follow the example of the premier leagues in Europe and split into two divisions of twenty clubs each with relegation and promotion introduced. Setting aside further discussion of relegation and promotion, the positive trajectory MLS is following is exciting to consider.

But what about the alternative?

It's hard imagining, but one must consider—especially with the history of the sport in North America—that MLS growth could stall or even go backward. Naysayers usually point out why they believe MLS won't become a top three global football league and why MLS will continue to lag behind the other four major North American leagues based on financials. They will seriously doubt that MLS can rival the world's best leagues, suggesting the following:

1. MLS doesn't feature team relegation and promotion; therefore, it cannot become a legitimate global soccer league. Without relegation and promotion, a soccer league is not valid.

2. It will require another thirty years before the quality of play in MLS reaches the levels currently seen in Europe. This is a familiar comment. It explains why many European players move to MLS late in their careers and thrive and why few North Americans play

in Europe. In addition, the USMNT does not play well in the quadrennial FIFA World Cup or the largely U23 Olympic Games.

3. Americans will never choose soccer over American football, baseball, basketball, or ice hockey. A small part of the market might, but those leagues have too much tradition, too many loyal fans, and cultural institutionalization.

4. North American children believe NFL, MLB, NBA, and NHL players will always make more money than soccer players, which means the most gifted natural athletes will pick other sports over soccer when it is time to specialize.

5. NCAA men's soccer is not as important as—or anywhere close to—NCAA football, men's and women's basketball, softball, volleyball, and baseball. Thus, soccer won't get a meaningful bump at the collegiate level fast enough to help MLS. The inability to develop local talent will always send the best overseas to European leagues.

6. The USMNT and Canadian Men's National Team will not reach the finals of the FIFA World Cup for at least another twenty years which means MLS won't receive a patriotic lift every four years. Translation? North Americans won't sense improvement from players in these two countries.

7. Ambitious European teams will continue promoting their brands in North America and selecting promising youngsters for their overseas academies. They will also sign the best American players in the future and build digital fan clubs in North America, thereby limiting MLS to a second-tier league.

8. The historic Apple deal, while groundbreaking for MLS, is not enough to overcome the long head start of preestablished leagues (NFL, MLB, NBA, NHL) and Europe's biggest premier leagues (EPL, La Liga, Serie A, Bundesliga, and Ligue 1) enjoy on the media front, in terms of media coverage, revenue from rights fees, ideal time slots, media rights deals, and deep partnerships with networks.

While the above offers a range of negative or contrarian approaches, there are numerous reasons to suggest MLS will actually deliver a very bright future, one setting the league on par with its North American and Premier League counterparts. These include:

1. The sophistication of North American marketers mixed with the population base of the United States and Canada (nearly 400 million people) creates valuable economies of scale difficult to achieve in England, Italy, Spain, Germany, or France when those countries operate independently. In short, the contiguous landmass of the United States and Canada and the combined populations of both countries provide MLS an attractive footprint to target for media, sponsorship, fan affinity, merchandise, streaming, ticket sales, and more.

2. What Inter Miami and Messi are achieving financially and statistically (on the pitch) is not going unnoticed by top players in European leagues. Said another way, Messi will not be the last great player still in their prime to choose MLS over enticing European and global options.

3. Much like Messi, David Beckham, as co-owner of Inter Miami, is also being watched by the top players who now might see a progression to ownership and enhanced wealth post-career from a move to MLS.

4. For most of the past two decades, studies about youth sport participation in both the United States and Canada shows soccer gaining more participants than the traditional mainstays of tackle football, ice hockey, and baseball. Tackle football and baseball defined many aspects of American culture for the last one hundred years, while ice hockey is the same for Canada, but as new generations are identified, they will "shift the paradigm" and underpin MLS as a legitimate member of the Big Five (NFL, NBA, MLB, NHL, MLS). A similar argument is true for basketball, whose number are also on the rise in both countries. Youth participation does not

automatically mean the creation of fans or ticket buyers, but it does drive a sport's role in popular culture, which has indirect impact on the business outcomes down the road.

5. Although linear television is fading in its influence, streaming, podcasts, and social media are all on the rise. These channels all include sports news content, and in just the last few years, the North American media now routinely include MLS when commenting on professional sports. The Big Four of the past is now the Big Five. That means MLS is legit and game results or MLS news are stories the average sport fan "sees" on a daily basis.

6. While the five biggest European soccer leagues are based around a limited number of major metropolitan cities (London, Manchester, Liverpool; Rome, Milan, Naples; Barcelona, Madrid; Berlin, Munich, Frankfurt, Stuttgart; Paris, Marseille), MLS features more than twenty-five major metropolitan markets in a spread-out geography that will continue to expand and build new fans. Indeed, there are many markets in North America where the MLS club is one of the biggest games in town (e.g., Columbus, Austin).

7. In stock market terms, MLS is still an investment (or growth) stock where investors see a very rich upside based on several promising trends including stadium attendance, merchandise sales, league and team sponsorships, and, most important, team profitability. Combined, these factors are dramatically driving MLS team valuations up and attracting a new generation of owners. The missing link of increased media audiences is right around the corner.

8. Technological advances, and the long-term Apple deal, bodes well for MLS especially since Apple technology appeals to a younger audience that prioritizes digital speed and accessibility. It doesn't hurt that Apple is the most valuable brand on the planet. Think about that. MLS has partnered with Apple at a deep, integrated level. Even the NFL, the top sport entertainment property in North America, has only partnered with Apple since 2022 and only for the halftime show of the Super Bowl.

9. Where other North American leagues (and the NCAA) have long relied on television rights fees to underpin revenue generation, MLS—with its deal with Apple—is not as tied to TV for the delivery of game product. They have made the move to streaming and digital ahead of the leagues they are chasing. This reality should keep MLS closer to the cutting edge when it comes to future fan engagement and puts it in a place to capture younger and nontraditional audiences. It also allows it to best cater to soccer fans who live outside of North America.

10. As MLS continues to grow, opportunities to engage hungry audiences in the Caribbean, Central America, and Mexico will give MLS advantages because this future fan base knows the game and is highly sophisticated when it comes to watching and discussing football. The fact that MLS media coverage and games are as available in Spanish as they are in English is a significant asset for the league to reach Spanish-speaking fans, both for those countries where soccer is the number-one game, like Mexico, or in others where soccer trails but has the ability to move up. For example, while MLB has a huge audience in the Dominican Republic, it is soccer, the global game, that resonates most loudly in many of the countries nearby and globally, suggesting an opportunity for MLS avidity.

In summary, the pros outweigh the cons.

Granted, the above dialogue is simplistic, but the different points of view are drawn from a deep analysis generated from the creation of this book. Taking things a bit further, it's fair to suggest any assessment of an organization must ask if the entity has the resources and leadership to consistently grow.

MLS does.

Its leadership, in particular, commissioner Don Garber, former president and deputy commissioner Mark Abbott, current deputy commissioner of MLS and president of Soccer United Marketing Gary Stevenson, former Soccer United Marketing president Kathy

Carter, executive vice president and chief communications officer Dan Courtemanche, and senior vice president of emerging ventures Chris Schlosser all have proven track records when it has come to making smart decisions, dedicated uses of resources, designing calculated growth, and surviving intense challenges.

To be sure, the league was on the ropes in the late 1990s early 2000s and the David Beckham experiment offered numerous risks. But it also delivered real rewards that were fully realized then (including Beckham's commitment to own an MLS team) and they continue to reveal themselves circa 2025.

The arrival of Leo Messi (and his amazing early MLS performances) is further proof the league is "there" and hovering on the precipice of elite global status. The development of team-identified youth academies will also help (in fact, Messi's son, Thiago, is already playing at the Inter Miami academy). It's a long way of suggesting we have no doubt MLS's leadership is aggressively designing future growth strategies, and we can only imagine what North America's premier soccer league will look like in 2035 and beyond.

From a league with few teams and massive annual losses during the late 1990s, the leaders at MLS not only showed they knew (and know) what they are doing, but also were (and are) capable of building what was once unimaginable. Major events across 2025–2028 will help. So will improved play on the pitch and continued investment from American sponsors.

MLS is rising and will continue doing so.

The MLS in 2010 versus 2025

My book, *Star-Spangled Soccer: The Selling Marketing and Management of Soccer in the USA*, was published in the spring of 2010 just as the fifteenth season of Major League Soccer got underway. The book covered the impact of the United States hosting the 1994 FIFA World Cup, including the crucial role it played in launching MLS, a mandate given to U.S. Soccer by FIFA for the privilege of hosting the Cup.

I grew up in England as a fanatical (and still am) Coventry City and England fan, still hanging onto England's 1966 World Cup win and Coventry's historic 1987 FA Cup triumph over Spurs. Defining moments in my soccer life (and my wife might say, life in general) included attending the 1984 Olympics and witnessing the potential power of soccer in the United States with a sold-out Rose Bowl for the Gold Medal Match between France and Brazil. Not long after I arrived back in the United States after completing an MBA and launching a sports marketing business with a firm belief soccer would explode in North America. It took a while, but it happened.

Some might say the measure of a successful and legitimate global soccer country is the quality of its professional league and the quality of players the country produces. If true, no one can argue that the United States is among the best in staging world-class mega events. It's in the DNA of the country, particularly evident with the Men's 1994 Cup and the 1999 Women's World Cup.

Still, launching a new soccer league is a completely different ball game. Our company (API Soccer) was a founding investor in the League, owning part of D.C. United for the first five seasons. Despite a delayed start that quelled a lot of the "buzz" from 1994, MLS started off well before entering a death spiral of falling attendance and cash calls that saw MLS on the brink of collapsing in 2001 (with investors heading for the hills). Only the deep pockets and blind (soccer) faith of the Hunts, Krafts, and Anschutzes saved it. Two teams were ultimately culled, and a new approach was taken to acquire even more soccer media rights.

Ostensibly, one of those gambles saved the league. New teams, stadiums, and investments followed, but the 2007 arrival of David Beckham was arguably the real catalyst for the adrenaline injection the League needed. Beckham delivered the one thing the league, investors, sponsors, and media desperately needed: confidence.

Confidence soccer was finally here to stay as an American sporting staple and that MLS could survive. Confidence that if investors bought a team and built a soccer-specific stadium (as they did in Columbus more than twenty-five years ago), fans would show up and fill the seats. In particular, NYCFC, backed by Manchester City (one of the richest and fastest-growing sides in the world) delivered on a promise (now realized) to build a desperately needed stadium in New York City. Confidence also came from fans that teams were well-funded and capable of going the distance. Confidence came from sponsors believing it was worth investing in clubs that can reach their targeted audiences.

The simplest way to view all of this is by noting the MLS ecosystem has seen franchise values rise from $30 million in 2010 to the $500 million paid by the thirtieth entrant San Diego or by learning LAFC was valued by *Forbes* at $1.2 billion and Messi's Inter Miami at $1.1 billion. These achievements tell a confident story of marketplace belief, one made even more tangible by the recent *Ted Lasso* phenomena.

It has not, however, happened in isolation. MLS has benefited greatly from the overall growth of interest in the Premier League, Champions League, U.S. Men's and Women's World Cup Campaigns, Liga Mx, Summer Tours, and every other soccer touchpoint that has permeated America in the past thirty years. Confidence is everything in sports, and soccer in the United States and MLS now have it. Not surprisingly, my follow-up to *Star-Spangled Soccer* is scheduled for spring 2025.

Afterword

Mark Abbott, former MLS President and Deputy Commissioner

When Canada, Mexico, and the United States host the FIFA World Cup in 2026, the world will witness just how much our sport is flourishing here in North America by every statistical measure. This will be just the latest example of the pivotal role that the World Cup has played in the development of soccer in the United States.

The modern era of professional soccer in the United States began with the launch of the North American Soccer League in 1967. The previous summer, the 1966 World Cup was played in England and the tournament culminated in the classic final between England and West Germany.

That match was broadcast on U.S. network television giving many sports fans in the United States their first exposure to the world's most popular sport. Also watching that day were a group of entrepreneurs including Lamar Hunt, owner of the Kansas City Chiefs, and later, one of the original MLS owners. Lamar, along with others, believed that the time was right to start a soccer league in America.

With the arrival of many of the sport's greatest stars in the mid-1970s, including Pelé and Franz Beckenbauer, the NASL experienced a few years of great success. Unfortunately, the league was not sustainable, and the NASL folded following the 1984 season.

It was against this backdrop that the leaders of U.S. Soccer decided to bid for the right to host the World Cup to help boost interest in soccer in the United States. FIFA agreed and on July 4, 1988, the United States was selected to host the 1994 World Cup with a requirement that the tournament be used as a catalyst to launch a new league.

The original idea was to start the league in 1992, so it would be in place prior to the World Cup. Although it's hard to imagine now, there were some doubts at that time whether there would be sufficient fan interest in a World Cup in the United States and an ability to sell out the matches.

The decision was made to focus on promoting the World Cup and to delay the debut of the league until after the tournament. The1994 World Cup was of course a tremendous success both on and off the field and, as hoped, generated significant interest among fans, broadcast companies, commercial sponsors, and potential owners as well as nearly twenty-five cities across the country in the plans for what was initially called Major League Professional Soccer.

In developing the original business plan for MLS, we had a unique opportunity to design a league from scratch. Our goal was to play the world's game supported by a modern and sustainable business structure.

We studied the established professional sports leagues in the United States as well as several international soccer leagues. We also conducted an extensive analysis of the North American Soccer League so that we could learn from both its successes and failures. In constructing the plan, we realized that we not only needed to build a league, but also elevate the sport itself. There was almost no infrastructure in place to operate a professional soccer league in the United States in the mid-1990s so we had to create it.

We were fortunate to attract an initial investor group that included some of the most accomplished businesspeople and sports team owners in the United States. They contributed not only their resources, but also their experience. They supported a bold vision to build a world-class league but were also clear-eyed about the challenge in front of us.

The initial launch of MLS in April of 1996 exceeded our expectations—there were record crowds in the ten MLS markets in the first few weeks and nearly eighty thousand fans packed Giants Stadium to watch the MLS All-Star game as part of a doubleheader with the FIFA World All-Stars playing Brazil.

Those first few months were fun, maddening, stressful, sometimes crazy, and often exhausting. We experienced moments of great exhilaration as the league we had planned had now become a reality—but at times, it also seemed surreal. There were challenges to be sure as we went from elation one day to a crisis the next. I think the inaugural MLS Cup best represents the highs and the lows of that first season—a magical match played in near hurricane conditions.

Both the magic and the hurricanes continued in the years that followed and it has been the ability to navigate between the two that has enabled MLS to grow and prosper. The fundamental principle behind the structure of MLS was to provide the league with the ability to change and innovate to manage new challenges and opportunities as they arise, effectively and efficiently. I believe the willingness to constantly evaluate the league's strategy and to pivot when required has been a hallmark of MLS since its inception and a key to its success. There are countless examples of this principle in action such as the creation of Soccer United Marketing to grow the commercial value of soccer, the changes to our player rules to facilitate the signing of players like David Beckham (and now Messi), and the commitment to build world-class soccer stadiums, to cite just a few. And there will be more to come.

At the last board meeting before I stepped down from my role as deputy commissioner at the end of 2022, I concluded my thoughts about the future of MLS with my favorite quote from Winston Churchill: "This is not the end. This is not the beginning of the end. This is the end of the beginning."

In this wonderful book, Rick Burton and Norm O'Reilly have captured the phenomenal progress of soccer in the United States and Canada since the 1994 World Cup. But they have also looked to the future and on that score, I have never been more optimistic.

ACKNOWLEDGMENTS

No modern book is generally printed without the author (or authors, in our case) expressing sincere appreciation for all who helped them summit their book-publishing mountain or, to use a soccer metaphor, in converting their penalty kick. Like others before us, our list is lengthy because for an industry-facing book like this, insights from industry leaders and those "who were there" were absolutely essential.

For numerous good reasons, the people listed below made this book possible.

First and foremost, we owe a great debt of gratitude to everyone at MLS who supported our collective effort and believed in the value of this book.

From Commissioner Don Garber, who graciously provided our foreword, to Executive Vice President, Chief Communications Officer Dan Courtemanche; Senior Vice President of Emerging Ventures, Chris Schlosser; Manager of Communications, Will Glenn; Chief of Staff, Nina Tinari; Peter O'Brien in corporate communications; and Michelle Nissen, executive assistant to the Commissioner, we owe you all a great debt of thanks.

We are also deeply indebted to *Sportico* columnist and good friend Kurt Badenhausen whose early expert efforts (including multiple informative graphs/charts) were hugely valuable. We also called on a number of other friends including former MLS executives Mark Abbott and Kathy Carter, authors Steven Mandis and Gary Hopkins, Orlando's Jarrod Dillon, San Jose's Gordon Kane, journalists/media members Scott French, Jeff Rusnak, David Sternberg, and other industry leaders such as Tom Anselmi, Gabriel Gabor, Ian McIntyre, Johnny Misley, Muralee Das, and Imran Choudry of T1 Futbol.

A super shout-out to future industry leader Arabella Titley who contributed wonderful material from Great Britain to the MLS expansion chapter while still only in high school. Arabella is author Steven Mandis's niece, and we were indeed fortunate to connect with Arabella as the book was in its final stages. And to broadcaster Philip Galati IV who did his senior honors thesis at Syracuse on "How Lionel Messi Is Rewriting the Past, Present, and Future of Professional Soccer in America." And thanks to Syracuse student Maxime Theriault for his observations on Football Manager.

As with all of our co-authored books, we reserve a very sincere "thank you" for Syracuse University's Margie Chetney who holds everything together for the sport management department in the David B. Falk College of Sport. Margie consistently fixes things and saves the day and so, this book honors her accordingly. As it does Falk College Dean Jeremy Jordan, who made it possible for one of the authors to spend a semester focused on this book.

Thanks too to Donna at the Clayton Hotel Ballsbridge in Ireland for making "the best pot of tea in Dublin." During an intense editing session, that "cuppa" saved the day.

We also would like to take the opportunity to recognize mentors who have enabled us to advance to the stage where we could even consider a book such as this. People like Mark Harrison, Bill Hallett, Judith Madill, Richard Pound, George Foster, Dick Strup, Jerry Schmutte, John Mellein, Myles Schrag, Dennis "Doc" Howard, and John Barrows, all of whom have given much more to us than we did for them.

We'd also like to thank Jennifer Unter of The Unter Agency for her representation and for connecting us with Lyons Press and the Globe Pequot Publishing Group. We would like to thank Rick Rinehart, Ken Samelson, Justine Connelly, Felicity Tucker, and Emily Natsios, who made all the difference in bringing this book to life.

Finally, and most importantly, we'd like to call out (with sincere thanks) our wives—Barb and Nadège—and wide-ranging families for their never-ending patience, support, and time as sounding boards.

Expert Perspective Biographies

Mark Abbott became the first employee of MLS in 1993 and was the principal author of the league's business plan. Over his thirty-year career with MLS, Abbott held a number of positions including president and deputy commissioner. He was responsible for a wide range of areas including player relations, competition, operations, communications, medical, legal, and finance. Together with Commissioner Garber, he also had responsibility for the league's expansion strategy.

Prior to joining MLS, Abbott was an associate at Latham and Watkins in Los Angeles and practiced corporate law. Abbott earned his law degree in 1989 from Boalt Hall School of Law at the University of California, Berkeley. While at Berkeley, Abbott was the managing editor of the *California Law Review*. Abbott is a 1986 graduate of Georgetown University, where he earned a Bachelor of Science Foreign Service degree in international economics, cum laude, and an honors certificate in international business diplomacy.

In 2023, Abbott received an appointment as a Distinguished Executive-in-Residence at Georgetown University. He has developed and co-teaches a class—Pro Sports and the Polis—that uses examples from the structure and operations of professional sports leagues to help better understand abstract concepts from political theory, theories of justice, and constitutional law. He also continues to serve as an advisor to MLS.

Tom Anselmi is an accomplished sports and entertainment executive. He was chief operating officer of Maple Leaf Sports & Entertainment for eighteen years, with business responsibility for all MLSE properties when Toronto FC was launched. His sports and entertainment background also includes Toronto's Skydome (now the Rogers Centre), Canuck Sports & Entertainment, Ottawa Senators, and Oilers Entertainment group.

Kurt Badenhausen is a sports valuations reporter at *Sportico*. Prior to joining *Sportico* he was a senior editor at *Forbes* where he worked from 1998 to 2021. He co-engineered *Forbes*'s annual sports team valuations and launched numerous initiatives at the company, including annual features on brand valuations, best banks, and top business schools. He profiled numerous athletes who go by one name: Serena, LeBron, Shaq, Danica, and others for the magazine.

Prior to joining *Forbes*, Badenhausen worked at *Financial World* magazine where his coverage focused on investing, mutual funds, and the business of sports.

A sports executive, **Kathy Carter** has blazed trails during her thirty-year career in sports, leading successful organizations, challenging the status quo across the sports industry. Until 2024, Carter was the CEO of LA28. In this role, she oversaw all aspects of the organization. Prior to being named CEO, Kathy led the commercial efforts for Team USA and the LA28 Olympic and Paralympic Games. She joined the organization in October 2018 and was only the third woman in the history of the Games to lead an Olympic and Paralympic Organizing Committee.

Prior to LA28, Carter served as president of Soccer United Marketing (SUM), Major League Soccer's (MLS) commercial subsidiary. Carter held several positions with SUM since she joined in 2003, including executive vice president and vice president of corporate marketing. Her career in the sports industry began with the 1994 FIFA World Cup, when she worked for the World Cup Organizing Committee. After the 1994 FIFA World Cup, Carter was a founding member of MLS and was instrumental in building the league from the ground up.

In addition to her roles as a soccer executive, Carter has been involved in developing women's soccer at the international level in her prior capacity as the U.S. representative on FIFA's Committee for Women's Football and the FIFA Women's World Cup. Additionally, Carter worked in tennis with the Tennis Masters Series. Carter has been recognized as the WISE Woman of the Year, a two-time winner of the *Sports Business Journal's* 40 Under 40 award, named to the New York Crain's 40 Under 40 list, and included on *Forbes's* list of The Most Powerful Women in Sports.

Imran Choudhry's drive for creativity, innovation, and outside-the-box thinking fuels his love for brand building. An innovative entrepreneur blessed with logic, intuition, and interpersonal skills, Imran shares twenty-plus years of professional experience leveraging data and strategy to build sponsorship campaigns for T1 clients. An insightful and versatile professional with an understanding of working with brands, NFPs, and properties, Imran brings to the table a well-rounded viewpoint and a propensity for perfection. Working across all industries, Imran manages teams on long-term strategies and quick turn campaigns of all sizes with a keen eye for strategy and evaluation.

Originally appointed vice president and partner in 2011, Imran has driven success for a long list of clients across all sectors and industries. His collaborators have included Allstate, BMW, Red Cross, Canada Soccer, Coca-Cola, CONCACAF, Esso, FIFA, Mattel, Nike, OLG, PlayStation, Visa, and more. Under Imran's leadership, the agency's work has been recognized locally and globally for dozens of awards.

With a lifelong passion for soccer, Imran launched T1 Futbol, a division of T1, focused on providing strategic marketing expertise for brands and properties wanting to build partnerships around one of the world's most inclusive sports. T1 Futbol builds exciting partnerships, creates meaningful experiences, and helps amplify brand stories.

Imran was the starting goalkeeper for the Yeomen Varsity Soccer team while at York University completing his Bachelor of Commerce—Marketing (Honours). Having coached for over thirty years at the grassroots level, Imran holds a National C license in coaching, putting it to good use coaching his three kids playing soccer. His son is a member of the Toronto FC Academy system, while his two daughters currently play for youth club Pickering FC.

Muralee Das is an associate professor of management at the Maine Business School, University of Maine. He teaches strategic decision making, human resource management, and sport management. In his previous appointment at Australia's Monash University, he taught corporation law and business law.

Muralee's teaching and research captures insights from his past corporate career as assistant general secretary (assistant chief executive officer) and director of human resources and services for the Asian Football Confederation (AFC). The AFC, part of Switzerland-based FIFA, is one of the world's largest sports governing organizations overseeing forty-seven countries. Muralee also served on the advisory board of the International Federation of Professional Footballers (FIFPro) Asia/Oceania division and was a general coordinator at the multi-sports Asian Games.

His research articles and case studies on sports gambling, fantasy sports regulation, artificial intelligence in sports, sports governance and corruption in global sports, and strategic management of basketball leagues have been published in numerous peer-reviewed journals.

Das received his PhD in management from the Melbourne Business School, University of Melbourne in Australia where he was the Ian Kirk Social Entrepreneurship Fellow. He earned a master's in commercial law from University of Melbourne, MBA from University of Nevada–Las Vegas, and a BBA from University of Iowa. Muralee, an Australian national and U.S. resident, was raised in Southeast Asia and has worked in the United States, Australia, and Asia.

Jarrod Dillon is the president of business operations for the Orlando City, Orlando Pride, and INTER&Co Stadium. He joined the organization January 3, 2022. He is responsible for the overall strategic business operations of each of the club's properties including Orlando City Soccer Club of Major League Soccer, the Orlando Pride of the National Women's Soccer League, the Orlando City Academy, the Orlando City Youth Soccer Network, and INTER&Co Stadium. Reporting directly to ownership, Dillon oversees a unified front office strategy for both Orlando City and Orlando Pride, working alongside both soccer operations teams to bring a best-in-class experience to fans and to the Orlando community.

Dillon joined Orlando City Soccer Club and the Orlando Pride after six years with Vinik Sports Group (VSG). Over his tenure with VSG, Dillon started as the club's executive vice president of sales and marketing before being promoted to chief marketing and revenue officer. In this role, Dillon was responsible for leading the revenue strategies for all VSG properties including the National Hockey League's Tampa Bay Lightning, AMALIE Arena, Yuengling Center, Identity Tampa Bay, Tampa Bay Sports, and third-party media rights for the University of South Florida Athletics. During his tenure, the Lightning were named ESPN's 2016 Franchise of the Year and were two-time finalists for *Sports Business Journal*'s Team of the Year (2016, 2021), amassing more than 240 consecutive sellouts.

Prior to his most recent experience in the NHL, Dillon worked with MLB's San Diego Padres and San Francisco Giants, as well as with the Oakland Raiders of the NFL, in roles encompassing ticket and suite sales, customer service, analytics, and corporate partnerships.

Scott French is a Southern California–based sportswriter who has covered professional soccer since the late 1970s, when he was in his teens, and extensively since 1991. A former senior editor at *Soccer America*, managing editor of *MajorLeagueSoccer Magazine*, assistant sports editor at the *Los Angeles Daily News*, and staff writer at *FourFourTwo USA*, he has covered the Galaxy since the club's inception, initially as beat writer for the *Long Beach Press-Telegram*.

He has also covered three World Cups, two Women's World Cups, three Olympics, and the 2000 European Championship, as well as all three women's professional leagues, APSL, USL, three professional indoor leagues, college and prep soccer, in addition to other sports.

Gabriel Gabor has been an award-winning communications and marketing executive for more than thirty years, specializing in sports, travel, and entertainment. Since 2006, he has served as a Miami-based senior consultant for Major League Soccer and its commercial arm, Soccer United Marketing. In this capacity, Gabor has worked as media officer for countless MLS Cups, MLS All-Star games, and the North American tours of some of the world's most recognized clubs, including Manchester United and FC Barcelona, and the national teams of Mexico, Argentina, and Brazil.

In addition, Gabor has served as media officer for the 2015 FIFA Club World Cup in Japan, the 2016 Cope América Centenario, and the last twelve editions of the CONCACAF Gold Cup—including four finals. Gabor, who also served as the NBA Latin America's director of communications (2001–2004) and vice president of communications for the Miami Fusion (1998–2001), specializes in venue media operations and player media training.

Gary Hopkins holds an MBA from Warwick Business School in the UK and a BA in Sports Science from Loughborough University. As former president and CEO of API Soccer and a managing director at Octagon, he has been involved in the commercial growth of soccer in the United States for over thirty years, working with U.S. Soccer, U.S. Youth Soccer, and Major League Soccer, along with consulting on Manchester City's U.S. growth and representing buyers in the acquisition of English National League Team Sutton United. He launched America's first full-color soccer magazine in the 1990s and once held the U.S. TV Rights to the English Premier League (then Division One.) He is the author of *Star-Spangled Soccer: The Selling, Marketing and Management of Soccer in the USA*, and is currently CEO of HSE Sport and Entertainment.

Gordon Kane has spent over thirty years in professional sports marketing and management. After initial positions in sales management at P&G, and brand management at Kraft, Gordon joined a small sports consultancy working with such clients as the NFL and the Indianapolis Motor Speedway. During World Cup 1994 (in the U.S.), he developed the marketing strategy for two sponsors—Sprint (in the U.S.) and Gillette (globally).

Kane ran sponsorship and marketing as director of marketing at the United States Olympic Committee for both the games in Atlanta and Salt Lake City, generating over $600 million in sponsorship revenue during that time period.

As an independent consultant (founding Victory Sports Marketing), he helped clients such as Deloitte, Chicago 2016 (Olympic bid), Manchester United, and Sunderland AFC. For the last three years he has served as head of partnership development for Major League Soccer's San Jose Earthquakes.

Steven Mandis holds a PhD and was an adjunct professor at Columbia Business school, where he taught in the finance and economics department. Previously, he worked at Goldman Sachs, Citigroup, and as a senior advisor to McKinsey.

His previous books include *What Happened to Goldman Sachs, The Real Madrid Way, What Happened to Serie A,* and *What Happened to the USMNT: The Ugly Truth about the Beautiful Game.* In 2015 and 2019, he competed in the Ironman World Championships in Kailua-Kona, Hawaii.

A native of Basildon, England, and one of the brightest head coaches in NCAA men's soccer, **Ian McIntyre** has led Syracuse University to unprecedented heights, including winning the 2022 NCAA national championship, since taking over the program in 2010.

A 1996 Hartwick graduate, McIntyre became the fifteenth coach in Syracuse soccer history and during his time at the helm, McIntyre has built the Orange into a consistent national contender. While McIntyre's 2015 squad needed to replace seven starters, it became the first No. 10 seed to win the ACC Tournament before advancing to the NCAA College Cup, a first in school history.

Elite-level players have consistently keyed the Orange's success with many advancing to MLS careers. McIntyre's recruiting classes have consistently been ranked in the top forty by *College Soccer News.*

Prior to taking the reins at Syracuse, McIntyre spent seven seasons (2003–2009) as the head coach at his alma mater, Hartwick College. He guided the Hawks to four ten-win seasons in his tenure and an appearance in the 2005 NCAA tournament.

McIntyre was also a standout player for the Hawks, earning NSCAA First Team All-America honors as a senior in 1995. He helped the program to two NCAA tournament berths and earned a reputation for clutch goal-scoring by notching game-winning goals in NCAA tournament victories against Rutgers and Boston University in 1993. He was enshrined in the Hartwick College Athletic Hall of Fame in 2001, his first year on the ballot.

Johnny Misley has been leading operations as Ontario Soccer's chief executive officer since 2015. A respected sports industry executive with more than thirty years of professional experience, Misley has been inspired by the power of sport and developmental process that can help athletes move from the playground to the podium.

Prior to his arrival at Ontario Soccer, Johnny served for twelve years as the executive vice president of hockey operations with Hockey Canada, leading Canada's national and Olympic Teams at World Championships and Olympic Games. While with Hockey Canada he was a part of the management group of fourteen gold medal championship teams that included four Olympic gold medals and one Paralympic gold medal with the men's and women's teams in 2002, 2006, and 2010 Winter Olympics and Paralympics.

Johnny also served for two years as the director of technical leadership for Canada's Own the Podium program where he led the technical leadership strategy for Winter and Summer Olympic sports. In this multi-sport leadership role, he held close working relationships with organizations such as Sport Canada, Canadian Olympic Committee, Canadian Paralympic Committee, Coaching Association of Canada, Canadian Sport Institutes, Canadian Interuniversity Sport, and all National Olympic Sport Organizations.

Jeff Rusnak is among an early generation of American journalists who began writing about soccer/football in the 1980s when it was widely dismissed as a "foreign" game in the United States. From 1985 to 2011 he was a print journalist based in Fort Lauderdale and originated a soccer column that was published each Sunday from 1997 to 2010 in the *Sun-Sentinel*. In 1998 he launched the weekly talk show *Radio Free Futbol* with Ray Hudson, and later hosted *The Fusion Post-Game Show* with Hudson following Miami Fusion home games.

Since 2008, he has served as director of development at the Art and Culture Center/Hollywood, where he produces the Open Dialogues documentary film series, winning a Regional Emmy Award in 2023 for *Black Voices | Black Stories* in the Diversity/Equity/Inclusion Long-Form category. He is seeking a publisher for his novel, *The Magnificent Marty Dale*, about an English soccer star who finishes his wayward career with a third-tier team in Florida.

David Sternberg is the co-head of media consulting at Range Sports, a division of Range Media Partners LLC. Prior to joining Range in 2023, David was founder and co-managing partner of Claygate Advisors, a Connecticut-based sports media consulting firm. He formed the company in August 2015 following a successful career in global sports media management at Fox Sports, Universal Sports, and Manchester United FC. Claygate's clients included the U.S. governing bodies for two major Olympic sports, two NBA teams, top-tier football clubs in England's Premier League and Italy's Serie A, two Division I athletic programs, and numerous emerging professional sports leagues.

At Manchester United, David oversaw strategy and operations for all the team's media businesses, including the MUTV television network, the manutd.com website, mobile apps and services, social media channels, and print publications. From 2013 to 2015 the club expanded the global reach of MUTV to ninety territories; launched official accounts on Twitter, Google+, Instagram, Sina Weibo, and WeChat; grew its total social media reach to over 100 million followers; secured new magazine, program, and book publishing partnerships; and introduced its first-ever suite of smartphone apps in partnership with regional mobile operators across Asia, the Middle East, and Africa.

Prior to joining Manchester United, David served for three years as the chief executive officer of Universal Sports, an Olympic-themed sports television network in the United States jointly owned by NBC Universal and Intermedia Partners. Before going to Universal Sports in April 2010, David spent nearly twelve years as a senior executive at Fox Sports, managing sports TV channels in the United States, Latin America, and the Middle East.

Selected References

Apple.com (2022), "Apple and Major League Soccer to Present All MLS Matches around the World for 10 Years, Beginning in 2023," June 14, found at: https://www.apple.com/newsroom/2022/06/apple-and-mls-to-present-all-mls-matches-for-10-years-beginning-in-2023/.

Associated Press (2023), "Apple Embraces Potential of Sports Streaming with MLS Deal," February 1, found at: https://www.usnews.com/news/sports/articles/2023-02-01/apple-embraces-potential-of-sports-streaming-with-mls-deal#:~:text=MLS%20will%20receive%20at%20least,significant%20involvement%20with%20a%20league.

Cline, Ernest (2011), *Ready Player One*. New York: Broadway Books.

CNBC (2021), "NFL Finalizes New 11-Year Media Deal, Amazon Gets Thursday Night Rights," March 18, found at: https://www.cnbc.com/2021/03/18/nfl-media-rights-deal-2023-2033-amazon-gets-exclusive-thursday-night.html.

Gladwell, Malcolm (2002), *The Tipping Point: How Little Things Can Make a Big Difference*. Boston: Back Bay Books.

Gladwell, Malcolm (2008), *Outliers: The Story of Success*. New York: Little, Brown.

Keith, Ted (2023), "First Bite of the Apple: What to Watch for as MLS Embarks on a Revolutionary Media Rights Deal," *Sports Business Journal*, March 13, Found at: https://www.sportsbusinessjournal.com/Journal/Issues/2023/02/13/In-Depth/apple-mls.aspx.

NBA (2023), "NBA and Meta Announce Multiyear Partnership Agreement," January 24, found at: https://www.nba.com/news/nba-and-meta-announce-multiyear-partnership-extension.

Negroponte, Nicholas (1995), *being digital*. New York: Alfred A. Knopf.

O'Reilly, Norm, and Burton, Rick (2022), *Business the NHL Way: Lessons from the Fastest Game on Ice*. Toronto: University of Toronto Press.

Telefonica (2022), "When Will 6G Arrive and What Progress Will it Bring?" December 22, found at: https://www.telefonica.com/en/communication-room/blog/when-will-6g-arrive-and-what-progress-will-it-bring/.

Other Notable Soccer Books

Ake, Catherine. (2024). The Harris Poll, "Interest in MLS Grows Along with the Launch of New Team," January 3, found at: https://theharrispoll.com/briefs/interest-in-mls-grows-along-with-the-launch-of-new-teams/.

Anderson, Chris, and Sally, David. (2013). *Why Everything You Know about Soccer Is Wrong*. New York: Penguin.

Bennett, K. J. M., Vaeyens, R., and Fransen, J. (2019). "Creating a Framework for Talent Identification and Development in Emerging Football Nations." *Science and Medicine in Football*, 3(1), 36–42.

Bradbury, J. C. (2021). "Financial Returns in Major League Soccer." *Journal of Sports Economics*, 22(8), 921–945.

Britt, Matthew. (2023). "What Are Smart Cities and Why Do We Need Them?" *Forbes*, August 18, found at: https://www.forbes.com/sites/honeywell/2023/08/18/what-are-smart-cities-and-why-do-we-need-them/?sh=5e037d876f69.

Buford, Bill. (1990/1991). *Among the Thugs*. New York: Vintage.

Eligon, John. (2005). "For M.L.S., the Sport's Future Is in the Eye of the Beholder," *New York Times*, November 11, D6, Found at: https://www.nytimes.com/2005/11/11/sports/soccer/for-mls-the-sports-future-is-in-the-eye-of-the-beholder.html.

Foer, Franklin. (2006). *How Soccer Explains the World: An Unlikely Theory of Globalization*. New York: Harper Perennial.

Hopkins, Gary. (2010). *Star-Spangled Soccer: The Selling, Marketing, and Management of Soccer in the USA*. New York: Palgrave MacMillan.

Jennings, Andrew. (2006). *Foul! The Secret World of FIFA: Bribes, Vote Rigging and Ticket Scandals*. London: HarperSport.

Kuper, Simon, and Szymanski, Stefan. (2009, 2012, 2014, 2018). *Soccernomics: Why England Loses; Why Germany, Spain, and France Win; and Why One Day Japan, Iraq and the United States Will Become Kings of the World's Most Popular Sport*. New York: Nation Books.

Mandis, Steven. (2016). *The Real Madrid Way*. Dallas: BenBella Books.

Mandis, Steven. (2021). *What Happened to the USMNT: The Ugly Truth about the Beautiful Game*. Chicago: Triumph Books.

McCormick, Bret. (2023). "New First Stadium," *Sports Business Journal*, November 27–December 3, 12–15.

Nicholson, Paul. (2019). Inside World Football, "Garber Says MLS Will Stick at 32 Teams as He Headlines Soccerex USA Opening Day," November 22, found at: https://www.insideworldfootball.com/2019/11/22/garber-says-mls-will-stick-32-teams-headlines-soccerex-usa-opening-day/.

Pelit, Asli. (2024). "Inter Miami, MLS, Will Lean into Messi Effect for 2024 Season." *Sportico*, February 21, found at: https://www.sportico.com/leagues/soccer/2024/inter-miami-mls-messi-2024-season-opener-1234767485/.

Sportico (2024). Valuations. Accessed March 24, 2024, from https://www.sportico.com/c/valuations/.

Sports Business Journal. (2024). "Best Sports Business Cities: Event Hosting," March 18–24, Vol. 26, No. 48, 16–54.

Sports Business Journal. "FIFA's Infantino Urges MLS Owners to 'Be Bold' to Grow League to Full Potential," April 15, found at: https://www.sportsbusinessjournal.com/Articles/2024/04/15/mls-fifa-gianni-infantino.

Tenorio, Paul. (2024). "Gianni Infantino Addressed MLS Owners' Meeting, a First for a FIFA President," *The Athletic*, April 9, found at: https://theathletic.com/5402848/2024/04/09/gianni-infantino-mls-owners.

Wahl, Grant. (2009). *The Beckham Experiment: How the World's Most Famous Athlete Tried to Conquer America*. New York: Crown Publishing.

Warren, K., and Agyemang, J. A. (2019). "Soccer in the United States." In S. Chadwick, D. Parnell, P. Widdop, and C. Anagnostopoulos (eds), *Routledge Handbook of Football Business and Management*. London: Routledge, 589–600.

Webster, F. E., Jr. (1965). "Modeling the Industrial Buying Process." *Journal of Marketing Research*, 2(4), 370–376.

Wrack, Suzanne. (2022). *A Woman's Game: The Rise, Fall, and Rise Again of Women's Soccer*, Chicago: Triumph Books.

INDEX

About the Authors

Rick Burton is the David Falk Distinguished Professor of Sport Management at Syracuse University and former faculty athletics representative (FAR) to the NCAA and ACC for Syracuse. He is a regular columnist for *Sports Business Journal* (with Norm O'Reilly) and the author of numerous books including *Business the NHL Way: Lessons from the Fastest Game on Ice*, *Sport Business Unplugged*, *20 Secrets to Success for NCAA Student Athletes* as well as two World War II historical novels, *The Darkest Mission* and *Into the Gorge*.

Having served as the former chief marketing officer for the U.S. Olympic Committee (USOC) and Commissioner of Australia's National Basketball League, his most recent novel, *Invisible No More* (co-authored with Scott Pitoniak), was published in December 2023. He lives with his wife in Upstate New York's Finger Lakes region.

Norm O'Reilly is the inaugural dean of the College of Business at the University of New England and director of the Center for Sport and Business Innovation there. Recognized as one of the leading scholars in the business of sports, he has authored or co-authored twenty books, including five with Rick Burton, and published more than 160 peer-reviewed management journal articles, most on sponsorship and the sport business.

For nearly twenty years, he has been minority owner and partner consultant with the Toronto-based agency, T1, with clients including Nike, UFC, Pepsi, Nissan, Esso/Exxon, Canadian Olympic Committee, Canadian Paralympic Committee, Hockey Canada, and many others. O'Reilly was "Assistant Chef de Mission" for the Canadian Paralympic

Team at the 2016 Paralympic Games in Rio, Brazil, and a member of the 2004, 2008, and 2010 Olympic Games Missions. He sits on the board of the Sponsorship Marketing Council of Canada and the research advisory group of ParticipACTION.